Web Site Design Simulation

ISBN 0-9721331-5-1

Michael Gecawich

Published by
Business Education Publishing
Box 8558
Warwick, RI 02888
U.S.A.

For more information, visit our Web site
at www.bepublishing.com

Copyright

Ultimate Fitness Web Site Design Simulation
Published by Business Education Publishing
Images provided by ThinkStock Images
(A division of Jupiter Media)

Author
Michael J. Gecawich

Editors
Kathleen Hicks
Monica Handy
Diane Silvia
Linda Viveiros
Lisa Wardle

Web Site Design Firm
Adaptive Minds, Inc.

Student Reviewers
Dan Dowding
Bill Nardone

Permissions
For permission to use materials from this text or the Ultimate Fitness Resource CD, please contact us by:

Tel:	888.781.6921	
Fax:	401.781.7608	
Web:	www.bepublishing.com	

Business Education Publishing
Box 8558 • Warwick, RI 02888 • U.S.A.

Preface

A Web site design simulation for Web site design students

Welcome to the Ultimate Fitness Web Site Design Simulation! This simulation was developed to provide Web site design students with an in-depth, real-world experience in developing a comprehensive business Web site using Web site design software.

Developed with the assistance of Web site design professionals, this simulation gives students a realistic view of how Web site designers work with clients to build comprehensive Web sites.

In the Ultimate Fitness Web Site Design Simulation, a scenario is created where the student assumes the role of a Web site designer for the Ultimate Fitness establishment. The simulation provides the necessary content, information, and instructions to build a variety of individual Web pages that will collectively make up a comprehensive Web site for Ultimate Fitness.

Ultimate Fitness will challenge Web site design, layout, and creativity skills by presenting a wide variety of individual Web pages to create. From the homepage to the resources page, the student will gain real-world practice and reinforcement in:

- Planning, building, and designing a Web site navigation format
- Planning, building, and designing a variety of individual Web pages
- Creating a consistent Web site design theme and style
- Working with hyperlinks
- Creating custom Web graphics using a Web graphic design software application
- Using your creativity and imagination
- Working with custom Web colors
- Using and formatting tables
- Developing a comprehensive, professional business Web site

It is assumed that the student already has a basic working knowledge of at least one Web site design software application. This simulation does not include step-by-step instructions that differentiate between different Web site design software applications. The material presented in the simulation is generic and can be completed using any Web site design software application.

This simulation is designed to be used in conjunction with the Ultimate Fitness Resource CD and with guidance provided by your instructor.

You are about to embark on an experience that will bring you as close as it gets to the real world of Web site design. *Get ready for Ultimate Fitness!*

Contents

Contents *(continued)*

Section 1: Introduction

1.1 Welcome to the Ultimate Fitness Web Site Design Simulation

In this simulation, you will assume the role of the Web site designer for Ultimate Fitness, a health and fitness establishment that provides a state-of-the-art health and fitness facility to its members. The Ultimate Fitness facility includes free weights, a variety of cardio machines, and offers a series of aerobic-style classes for its members to attain their fitness goals. Ultimate Fitness is a well-established health and fitness center that has experienced steady growth in acquiring new members since opening its doors in 1998. A more detailed description of the Ultimate Fitness establishment is provided in Section 2.

Why Ultimate fitness needs your Web site design skills

With the explosion in popularity of the Internet, a number of Ultimate Fitness employees, current members, and potential new members recommended that Ultimate Fitness establish a Web site. In response to these requests, Ultimate Fitness has decided to create a Web site which will serve as a resource for current and potential new members to access an overview of the Ultimate Fitness facility, membership pricing and specials, and contact information.

1.2 Your role as the Ultimate Fitness Web site designer

Using your creativity, strategic planning, and Web site design skills, you will design and build the entire Web site for Ultimate Fitness. Once completed, the Web site will be showcased by Ultimate Fitness to its current members and to attract potential new members.

Throughout this simulation, you will be provided with step-by-step guidance and instructions to build the Ultimate Fitness Web site. To help you build the Web site, a variety of images and documents are provided on the Ultimate Fitness Resource CD. More information about how to use the Ultimate Fitness Resource CD is provided in Section 3.

1.3 The skills you will be using in this simulation

The following is a list of the skills you will be using throughout this simulation:

- Planning, designing, and building a Web site navigation structure
- Creating and designing Web site buttons
- Web page layout and design
- Using e-mail and graphic image hyperlinks
- Using and formatting tables
- Producing and editing Web graphic images

- Technical writing
- Critical thinking
- Planning and decision-making
- Establishing a professional business Web presence
- The ability to use Web design skills to complete a comprehensive real-world Web site design project

1.4 Prerequisite knowledge to complete this simulation

This simulation is designed for all skill levels of Web site design. It is appropriate for the beginner, intermediate, and advanced user. However, it is assumed that the student has a basic working knowledge of the following skills:

- Proficiency in using a Web site design software application such as Microsoft FrontPage®, Macromedia Dreamweaver®, or Adobe GoLive® to design a Web site
- Proficiency in using a Web graphic design software application such as Microsoft Image Composer®, Adobe Photoshop®, or Macromedia Fireworks®

1.5 What you will need to complete this simulation

To complete this simulation, you will need the following:

- The Ultimate Fitness Resource CD installed on your computer
- A Web site design software application such as Microsoft FrontPage®, Macromedia Dreamweaver®, or Adobe GoLive®
- A Web graphic design software application such as Adobe Photoshop® or Microsoft Image Composer®
- Access to the Internet (recommended)
- Basic working knowledge of building a Web site
- Adobe Reader® software installed on your computer (can be downloaded for free from *http://www.adobe.com/products/acrobat/readstep2.html*)

1.6 Web page design software notes

This book is designed to be used with any Web page design software application. The simulation does not include instructions specific to any one particular Web site design software application. *It is important to note that some of the instructions and features required by the student may need to be modified according to the specific software used.*

This simulation can be completed using the design mode (point and click) interface available with most Web site design software applications or by using HTML coding.

1.7 Quick summary of the individual parts of this simulation

Below is a brief overview of the individual Web pages you will design and build in order to complete the Ultimate Fitness Web Site Design Simulation:

Summary of the individual parts in this simulation:

Part 1:   Getting Started by Planning and Organizing Your Web Site
Part 2:   Design and Build the Shared Navigation Areas
Part 3:   Design and Build the Homepage
Part 4:   Design and Build the Facilities Page
Part 5:   Design and Build the About Us Page
Part 6:   Design and Build the Membership Plans Page
Part 7:   Design and Build the Fitness Tips Pages
Part 8:   Design and Build the Class Schedule Page
Part 9:   Design and Build the Contact Us Page
Part 10: Design and Build the Resources Page

1.8 Installing the Ultimate Fitness Resource CD

This simulation is designed to be completed using this book in conjunction with the Ultimate Fitness Resource CD. The Ultimate Fitness Resource CD must be installed on your computer before beginning the simulation.

Installation instructions are provided in the file titled *"Install Instructions"* located on the Ultimate Fitness Resource CD.

1.9 A note to the instructor

This simulation is designed to be completed as an independent, self-paced project for the student, with guidance and facilitation provided by the instructor. It is recommended that the instructor become familiar with the simulation prior to administering it to students in a classroom environment.

This simulation is designed to allow students to exercise their own creativity and design abilities in constructing a comprehensive Web site from scratch. Although there are specific guidelines and instructions the student must follow in developing the Ultimate Fitness Web site, the end result will be unique for each student. Hence, there is no answer key to accompany this book.

To assist the instructor in administering and evaluating the simulation, a variety of resource materials are provided on the Ultimate Fitness Resource CD. The instructor resources available are described in *Section 3: Using this Book and the Ultimate Fitness Resource CD*.

> **Note:** Please see the Instructor's Guide (available on the Ultimate Fitness Resource CD) for a complete description of the instructor resources available for this simulation.

Section 2: Getting to Know Your Client

2.1 The importance of getting to know your client

When a business hires a Web site designer to build a Web site, an initial meeting, either face-to-face, over the phone, or by e-mail, takes place between the two parties. The purpose of this initial meeting is for the Web site designer to gather necessary background information about the client's business, to find out what type of information the client wants on the Web site, and to establish what type of Web presence or image the client wants to convey through the Web site.

The type of business the client is engaged in usually determines the overall look and feel that the Web site designer decides to incorporate into the Web site. For instance, a Web site for a comic store may have a fun, more colorful design, whereas a life insurance company may have a more serious, professional corporate design on its Web site.

This section introduces you (the Web designer) to your client, Ultimate Fitness.

2.2 Background information about Ultimate Fitness

Review the background information shown on the following page to familiarize yourself with your client. Knowing your client will allow you to begin thinking about the look and feel of the Web site you will be creating.

Review the background information provided on the next page

Review the information given below to become familiar with Ultimate Fitness ▼

Ultimate Fitness Background Information

Company Name: Ultimate Fitness

Company Slogan: The Ultimate Health and Fitness Center

Description of the Company: Ultimate Fitness is a health and fitness establishment that provides a state-of-the-art health and fitness facility to its members. The Ultimate Fitness facility includes free weights, a variety of cardio machines, and offers a series of aerobic-style classes for its members to attain their fitness goals. Ultimate Fitness is a well-established health and fitness center that has experienced steady growth since opening its doors in 1998.

The Ultimate Fitness Mission Statement: To provide state-of-the-art fitness equipment, programs, and support to help individuals maximize and achieve their fitness goals.

Address and Contact Information:
350 Park Avenue
New York, NY 10019
Phone: 1.888.757.4856
Fax: 1.888.757.4987
E-mail: contact@uf-online.com
Web site address: http://www.uf-online.com

Hours of Operation:
Monday – Friday 7 am – 10 pm
Saturday 8 am – 6 pm
Sunday 8 am – 5 pm

The Facility: The Ultimate Fitness facility consists of more than 20,000 square feet of health and fitness equipment space. The facility consists of one free weight gym area, two aerobics rooms, a cardio room, a sauna room, and Jacuzzi pool. There are also separate men's and women's locker rooms that contain lockers, changing rooms, and shower areas.

About the Customers of Ultimate Fitness: Members of Ultimate Fitness consist of both men and women ranging in age from 14 to 65 years old. The average age of a customer is 32 years old. The majority of the members are working-class people and students who utilize the Ultimate Fitness facility as a place to work out and stay physically fit.

Intended Target Audience of the Ultimate Fitness Web Site: Current Ultimate Fitness members and potential new members.

Section 3:
Using this Book and
the Ultimate Fitness
Resource CD

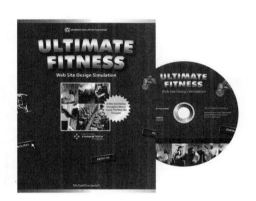

3.1 Understanding the format of this book

Each part of this simulation has been organized into an easy-to-read, step-by-step format. As previously mentioned, this simulation is designed to be used with any Web site design software application. This simulation does not include instructions specific to any one particular Web site design software application. It is assumed that the student has a basic working knowledge of using and working with Web site design software.

What follows is a brief explanation of the individual sections that make up each part of this simulation. Read it thoroughly to help you become familiar with the format and design of the book.

Each part of this simulation is organized using the format shown below.

Approximate Completion Time:

At the start of each new part of this simulation is the approximate amount of time it should take you to complete that section.

The total amount of time it should take you to complete this simulation is 20-32 hours. The completion time may vary based on your Web design skills and background knowledge.

Task and Purpose:

This section defines the task to be completed and provides the purpose and objectives for each part of the simulation.

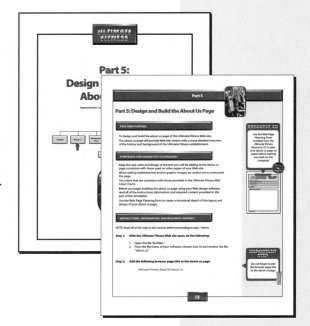

Strategies and Design Tips to Consider:

This section provides Web design tips, layout advice, and ideas and suggestions to consider before creating each Web page. By reading this section, you will get a clear idea of how to design an attractive, professional Web page.

Instructions, Information, and Required Content:

This section provides step-by-step instructions and specifications as to the content and information required to be included in each part of the simulation. This section also provides instructions on what Web design software features to include or apply to specific parts of each page.

3.2 Sidebar margin notations

Throughout this book, there are sidebar margin icons that provide the Web designer with additional tips, advice, reference charts, and assistance with each part of the simulation. Each sidebar margin icon is described below.

Sidebar Margin Icons

DESIGN TIP

Provides additional Web site design tips and advice that pertain to individual parts of the simulation.

RESOURCE CD

This icon is provided to alert you to utilize the Ultimate Fitness Resource CD to help build certain parts of each Web page in the simulation.

WEB FACT

Provides the reader with Web site facts that are relevant to certain parts in the simulation.

IMPORTANT STEP !

This icon alerts the reader to important steps in each part of the simulation.

QUICK REFERENCE COLOR CHARTS				

Ultimate Fitness RGB Web Color Chart

Color	Blue	Black	Grey	White
Red (R)	18	0	102	255
Green (G)	52	0	102	255
Blue (B)	90	0	102	255

Ultimate Fitness Hexadecimal Values Web Color Chart

Color	Hexadecimal Values
Blue	Hex={12, 34, 5A}
Black	Hex={00, 00, 00}
Grey	Hex={66, 66, 66}
White	Hex={FF, FF, FF}

This icon appears at the conclusion of each section to remind you to double-check your Web site and to make any necessary changes before moving on in the simulation.

Provides the reader with a quick reference to the Web colors that were used to develop the Ultimate Fitness logo.

This icon will appear at steps in the simulation where a hyperlink is required.

3.3 Using the Ultimate Fitness Resource CD

The Ultimate Fitness simulation is designed to be used in conjunction with the Ultimate Fitness Resource CD. The Ultimate Fitness Resource CD must be installed on your computer before you begin the simulation.

Installation instructions are provided on the Ultimate Fitness Resource CD.

Install the Ultimate Fitness Resource CD on your computer prior to beginning the simulation.

Contents of the Ultimate Fitness Resource CD:	
Accessed from the following folder	**Description**
Logos	Ultimate Fitness logo style files. Includes a printable document of all logo styles (file name "*View All Logo Styles*").
Fitness Images	Contains 65 high-resolution fitness-related photos. All images are in JPEG format. Includes a printable document to view all of the fitness images provided on the CD (file name "*View All Images*").
Student Documents	Printable documents including Color Charts, Web Page Planning Form, and Completion Timeline Table
*Instructor Resources	Instructor resources include an instructor's guide, grading rubrics, grading forms, completion timeline table, color charts, and other handouts.

*See the Instructor's Guide provided on the Ultimate Fitness Resource CD for a complete description of the resources available to the instructor.

The individual contents of the CD are explained on the following pages.

3.4 Contents of the Ultimate Fitness Resource CD

Ultimate Fitness Logo Styles

Since Ultimate Fitness is already an established business, you will be required to use a predesigned Ultimate Fitness logo in your Web site. The Ultimate Fitness Resource CD includes 32 different Ultimate Fitness logo styles to choose from. *You must choose one logo style to use in your Web site.*

The logos come in two different sizes: large and small. The logos are in high-resolution, JPEG (*Joint Photographic Experts Group*) format.

The logos are located under the folder titled "*logos*" installed from the Ultimate Fitness Resource CD. You can print a copy of all of the logo styles by opening the document titled "*View All Logo Styles*" located in the "*logos*" folder.

There are 32 Ultimate Fitness logo styles to choose from on the Ultimate Fitness Resource CD

The Ultimate Fitness logos can be accessed from the following directory:

<drive letter>:\Ultimate Fitness Resource CD\Logos

Fitness-Related Images by ThinkStock Images

The Ultimate Fitness Resource CD includes a variety of fitness-related images for you to use on each page in your Ultimate Fitness Web site. All of the images included on the resource CD are high-resolution photo quality and are in JPEG (*Joint Photographic Experts Group*) format. The images are located under the folder titled "*Fitness Images.*" You can print a copy of all of the fitness images by opening the document titled "*View All Images*" located in the "*Fitness Images*" folder.

Note: The images can be resized and customized by opening them in any Web graphic design software.

There are 65 high-resolution, fitness-related images on the Ultimate Fitness Resource CD.

The fitness images can be accessed from the following directory:

<drive letter>:\Ultimate Fitness Resource CD\Fitness Images

Note: The images included on the Ultimate Fitness Resource CD are copyrighted by Business Education Publishing and ThinkStock Images. You may use the images to help you build the Ultimate Fitness Web site only. The images are intended for non-commercial, classroom use only. Use in any other form is strictly prohibited and is a violation of copyright law.

Web Page Planning Form

It is recommended that you plan each page of your Ultimate Fitness Web site using the Web Page Planning Form provided on the Ultimate Fitness Resource CD. This document is titled *"Web Page Planning Form"* and is located in the folder titled *"Student Documents"* on the resource CD. It is recommended that you open and print several copies of the Web Page Planning Form before you begin the simulation.

Note: All of the documents included on the Ultimate Fitness Resource CD are in PDF (*Portable Document Format*) format.

Use the Web Page Planning Form to plan and sketch each Web page you build in the simulation.

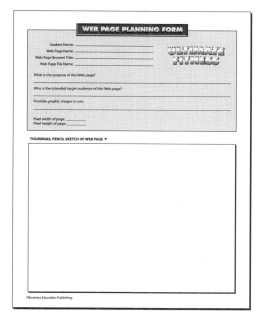

It is recommended that you open and print several copies of the Web Page Planning Form before you begin the simulation.

The Web Page Planning Form can be accessed from the following directory:

<drive letter>:\Ultimate Fitness Resource CD\Student Documents

Ultimate Fitness Web Color Charts

Colors that you see on a Web site are comprised of three colors: Red, Green, and Blue. These are commonly referred to as RGB. The colors that were used to create the Ultimate Fitness logos can be easily duplicated using any Web site design software application.

To help you establish a color scheme for your Ultimate Fitness Web site, the Ultimate Fitness Resource CD includes a printable document titled "*Color Charts*" located in the folder titled "*Student Documents*." It is recommended that you open and print the color chart before you begin the simulation.

The Ultimate Fitness Color Charts will allow you to use colors in your Web site that are identical to the colors used to create the Ultimate Fitness logo styles.

It is recommended that you open and print the color chart before you begin the simulation.

**ULTIMATE FITNESS
QUICK REFERENCE COLOR CHARTS**

Ultimate Fitness RGB Web Color Chart

Color	Blue	Black	Grey	White
Red (R)	18	0	102	255
Green (G)	52	0	102	255
Blue (B)	90	0	102	255

Ultimate Fitness Hexadecimal Values Web Color Chart

Color	Hexadecimal Values
Blue	Hex={12, 34, 5A}
Black	Hex={00, 00, 00}
Grey	Hex={66, 66, 66}
White	Hex={FF, FF, FF}

©Business Education Publishing

The Color Charts document can be accessed from the following directory:

<drive letter>:\Ultimate Fitness Resource CD\Student Documents

Completion Timeline Table

To help you manage your time while working through the simulation, you can use the Completion Timeline Table as a guide. The Completion Timeline Table provides the approximate number of hours it should take you to complete each part of the simulation. This document is titled "*Completion Timeline Table*" and is located in the folder titled "*Student Documents*" on the resource CD.

The Completion Timeline Table provides the approximate number of hours it should take to complete each part of the simulation.

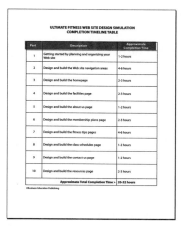

ULTIMATE FITNESS WEB SITE DESIGN SIMULATION
COMPLETION TIMELINE TABLE

Part	Description	Approximate Completion Time
1	Getting started by planning and organizing your Web site	1-2 hours
2	Design and build the Web site navigation areas	4-6 hours
3	Design and build the homepage	2-3 hours
4	Design and build the facilities page	2-3 hours
5	Design and build the about us page	1-2 hours
6	Design and build the membership plans page	2-3 hours
7	Design and build the fitness tips pages	4-6 hours
8	Design and build the class schedules page	1-2 hours
9	Design and build the contact us page	1-2 hours
10	Design and build the resources page	2-3 hours
	Approximate Total Completion Time >	20-32 hours

©Business Education Publishing

The Completion Timeline Table can be accessed from the following directory:

<drive letter>:\Ultimate Fitness Resource CD\Student Documents

Instructor Resources

The Ultimate Fitness Resource CD also includes a variety of resources available to the instructor. The instructor resources are located in the folder titled "*Instructor Resources*" on the Ultimate Fitness Resource CD.

Note: Each of the resources listed below are discussed in more detail in the Instructor's Guide provided on the resource CD.

The following resources are available to the instructor:

- Certificate of Completion
- Color Charts
- Completion Timeline Table
- Grading Rubrics
- Grading Form
- Instructor's Guide
- Printable handout of all of the Ultimate Fitness logo styles available on the resource CD
- Progress Checklist Form
- Printable handout of all of the fitness images available on the resource CD
- Printable handout of the Ultimate Fitness Web Site Navigation Flowchart
- Web Page Planning Form

All of the instructor resources can be accessed from the following directory:

<drive letter>:\Ultimate Fitness Resource CD\Instructor Resources

Section 4:
Overview of the
Ultimate Fitness Web Site

4.1 The Web site needs of Ultimate Fitness

With the explosion in popularity of the Internet, a number of Ultimate Fitness employees, current members, and potential new members recommended that Ultimate Fitness establish a Web site. In response to these requests, Ultimate Fitness has decided to create a Web site which will serve as a resource for current and potential new members to access an overview of the Ultimate Fitness facility, membership pricing and specials, and contact information.

4.2 Intended goals of the Ultimate Fitness Web site

Ultimate Fitness would like its new Web site to accomplish the following:

- To have a Web site that services the intended target audience of Ultimate Fitness: current Ultimate Fitness members and potential new members
- To provide existing members a place to view the personal training and aerobics class schedule online
- To let potential new members learn more about the Ultimate Fitness facility
- To let potential new members learn about membership rates and specials
- To provide existing and potential new members with a place to access free workout routines, nutrition tips, and fitness-related resources to help them achieve their fitness goals
- To build brand awareness with existing and potentially new Ultimate Fitness members
- To give existing and potential new members access to Ultimate Fitness employees to ask a question, submit feedback, or inquire about the facilities and services

The Web presence and image Ultimate Fitness would like to project:

Ultimate Fitness wants to project a friendly, professional image to its members to show them that Ultimate Fitness is a clean, comfortable, pleasing place to work out and stay fit.

4.3 How the Ultimate Fitness Web site will be organized and structured

The Ultimate Fitness Web Site Navigation Flowchart shown below illustrates how the pages of the Ultimate Fitness Web site will be structured and organized. You should use this chart as a guide when planning and designing your Ultimate Fitness Web site.

Ultimate Fitness Web Site Navigation Flowchart

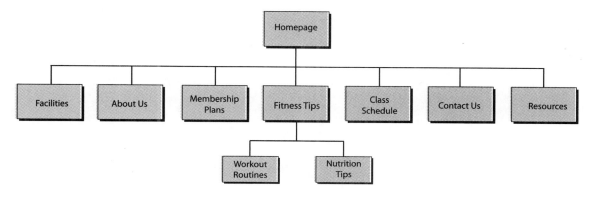

When you complete the simulation, the Ultimate Fitness Web site will include the following ten pages:

1. The Homepage
2. The Facilities Page
3. The About Us Page
4. The Membership Plans Page
5. The Fitness Tips Main Page

6. The Workout Routines sub-page
7. The Nutrition Tips sub-page
8. The Class Schedule Page
9. The Contact Us Page
10. The Resources Page

Section 5:
Web Site
Design Rules

5.1 The importance of following Web site design rules

Whether you're an experienced Web site designer or you're just getting started, the following are a few fundamental Web site design rules that will help you in the preparation and design of each Web page in the Ultimate Fitness simulation. Careful preparation, planning, and following the rules presented in this section will enable you to produce professional, attractive Web pages that you will be proud to show to others.

For starters, let's take a look at what makes a well-designed Web site effective.

A well-designed Web site should:

- be attractive and pleasing to look at and read.
- be well organized.
- be self-explanatory (the user should not have to look too far to know the message each Web page is conveying).
- contain text and graphics that are carefully linked to each other.
- contain design and content that are appropriate for the targeted audience.

5.2 Web site design rules

The following are some fundamental Web site design rules to adhere to as you produce each Web page throughout the simulation. *It is stongly recommended that you carefully read and review each rule before proceeding with the simulation.*

Rule#1: Your Web Site Should be Easy to Read and be Consistent Throughout

One of the most important Web design rules is to assure that your Web site is easy to read. This encompasses all possible elements of a Web site including navigational structure, color, text, graphics, backgrounds, borders, and hyperlinks.

To create a Web site that is easy to read, your Web site should: (*each of the areas presented below are discussed in more detail later in this section*)

- include a navigational structure that is easy to navigate.
- include a complementary color scheme.
- include graphics that are consistent in look and feel throughout the Web site.

WEB DESIGN RULES

- include text that is consistent in size, color, alignment, and is easy to read.
- include hyperlinks that work properly and are easily accessible to the user.
- not contain background colors that make the text hard to read or put a strain on the user's eyes.
- never change anything in the Web site just for the sake of change. Unless it's warranted, keep the look and feel of all of the elements in your Web site the same.

Rule #2: Know Your Target Audience

Determine the single most important message that your Web site should convey by asking yourself: If my Web site visitor carries away one main idea or concept, what do I want it to be? The answer will be the central focus theme that should determine your entire Web site's design.

When designing a Web site, it is important to know who your target audience is. In reference to Web sites, a target audience is any potential interested visitor to the Web site. When considering the design of a Web site, factors such as age, gender, and location should be considered.

Rule #3: Make Your Web Site's Navigation User-Friendly

A Web site should be easy to navigate. A user should not have to "guess" or "hunt" for hyperlinks or information. The Web site should present the user with a design that allows users to move from one page to another easily. A general rule of thumb to follow is to "spoon feed" your audience. In other words, anticipate that users know nothing about your site's subject area and build it from there.

Remember that it is more important that your Web site navigational elements are easy to read and understand than to have "flashy" effects.

A general rule to consider is this: Web site visitors should be able to find what they are looking for in your site within three mouse clicks. If not, visitors will likely click off your site as quickly as they clicked on.

Rule #4: Use White Space

White space is the area of a Web page that does not include text or graphics. Some Web sites include so much text and graphic images that they appear cluttered making it difficult for users to navigate and understand the main points of the Web site. A general rule of thumb is to include enough white space between text and images to allow users to read and "breathe" between different elements on your Web pages.

WEB DESIGN RULES

Rule #5: Determine Your Web Site's Page Size

The size of a user's Web browser window is probably one of the biggest headaches a Web designer will encounter. The trouble is that not everyone has the same size monitor running at the same resolution. To make things worse, different Internet browsers have different viewable screen areas.

Good Web designers understand that users can set their viewable screen settings to different sizes. A Web page with pixel width set too high will cause some users to have to scroll to the right or "off the screen" to read an entire Web page. This can cause Web users to become frustrated and navigate away from your site. To avoid users having to scroll to the right or too far down on a Web page, you must set your Web page size at the proper width and height. To do this, let's take a look at the possible monitor resolution sizes available.

The possible monitor screen resolution sizes are as follows:

640 x 480 pixels
800 x 600 pixels
1024 x 768 pixels (*most commonly used*)
1152 x 870 pixels

Since most Web visitors these days use a minimum resolution size of 800 x 600 pixels and either use Internet Explorer® or Netscape® Navigator Web browsers, a safe page size to work with is one that is set to be no more than 800 pixels wide and 600-900 pixels tall.

Rule #6: Lay Out Your Web Pages Using Tables

Using invisible tables to control the layout of your Web page can be useful in many ways. If you just simply place text on your Web page, it may look good in your Web browser, but if you change the size of your browser window, the text will re-flow to fill your browser window. This can ruin the appearance of your Web page leaving a non-professional impression with the user.

One way to give you more control over the layout and make your Web page design more interesting is to use tables.

Tables can be used to control many aspects of the Web page. They can be used to place text into columns, images next to text, navigation buttons in rows or columns, and many more things.

As discussed in Rule #5 above, you will need to pay attention to the pixel width of your tables. A safe width to use is 785 pixels or less. If you use a table that contains two or more columns, you will need to set the cell space accordingly so that they do not exceed the pixel width of your page.

WEB DESIGN RULES

Rule #7: Use Fonts That Will Display Correctly

Applying different fonts and typefaces in Web site design is not as simple as it is in print design. For example, let's say you would like your Web page's text to display in the typeface Avant Garde. In order for your Web pages to actually appear in this typeface, your visitors must have the Avant Garde typeface installed on their computers. If your visitors do not have this typeface, your Web pages will look completely different than what you intended.

The only way to have a typeface display exactly as you intend it to display on a Web page, is to put the typeface in a graphic image.

To avoid typefaces displaying incorrectly, you should use a font that comes pre-installed on all computers.

Because they are installed on most computers, the following is a list of Web safe fonts to use when designing Web pages:

Arial
Courier
Georgia
Helvetica
Times or Times New Roman
Verdana

Rule #8: Keep Text Consistent Throughout Your Web Site

For a professional looking Web site, follow the Web site text guidelines shown below:

- Do not make your text too small or too large. Avoid using a text size smaller than 8 points or larger than 14 points. Text that is too small is hard to read and text too large will give the appearance that you are "shouting" at your visitors.

- Keep the alignment of the body text to the left, not centered. Center-aligned text is best used in headlines. You want your visitors to be comfortable with what they are reading, and the standard format that people are accustomed to reading is left-aligned text.

- Text links should be unique and not look the same as any other text in your Web pages. A standard rule will keep this from happening. Since most hyperlinked text appears as an underlined typestyle, avoid underlining any text in your Web site (unless it is a hyperlink). In addition, make the color of hyperlinked text different than non-linked text to avoid confusing your visitors.

- Keep the color of your text consistent throughout your Web site. If you use one color for headlines and another for body text, keep this color scheme the same on all Web pages.

WEB DESIGN RULES

Rule #9: Research Competitor Web Sites

Before you begin designing your Web site, take the time to visit other similar Web sites. Compare and contrast the different layout, text, graphics, and color scheme used. This will help you to establish a Web site design structure that is compatible with the rest of the industry.

Rule #10: Establish a Professional Identity

When businesses communicate by means of a Web site, they rely heavily on the site's look and design to convey their intended message and identity to users.

Rule #11: Proofread for Spelling, Grammar, and Design

Nothing spoils a well-designed Web page more than a typo. When you are nearing the completion of each Web page, take the time to proofread it for spelling, grammar, and design. Are there any misspelled words? Do the sentences make sense? Did you leave out any required text or design elements?

A good piece of advice is to have one or two people review your Web site. They will often find an error or omission that you did not see. Ask them to check for spelling, grammar, punctuation, and language style.

Rule #12: Revise, Revise, Revise

Designing a Web site is much like writing an essay. It almost never comes out right the first time around. Look at the starting point of each Web page you design as just that—a starting point. Preview your Web pages frequently as you build them. Continually look for design and content inconsistencies, and make any necessary additions and deletions to obtain a professional, well-designed finished product.

Rule #13: Create a Well-Designed Web Site Architecture

After you review the content of your Web site, you need to decide on the framework or structure of the site and how it is all going to fit together. In the field of Web design, this is commonly referred to as Web site architecture or structure.

This is a very important stage as this is where you develop the layout that will determine how your Web site visitors will move from point A to point B in your Web site.

Later in the simulation, you will see that an organizational scheme has been created for you to use to develop the organizational structure of your Ultimate Fitness Web site.

WEB DESIGN RULES

Rule #14: Use Consistent Graphics

Graphic images help illustrate a Web page's message. When using graphic images, you should always use the same style of graphics throughout your Web site. For instance, if you are using photographic-quality images on your homepage, other graphics that appear on different pages throughout your Web site should also be photographic-quality images. Similarly, if you are using cartoon-like images on one page, they should be used on all pages throughout your Web site. Using different style images can confuse Web site visitors and create an unprofessional appearance.

The most common graphic formats supported by Web browsers for graphics are JPEG and GIF.

The JPEG (*Joint Photographic Experts Group*) format is usually used for photos where there are lots of subtle color changes and detail.

The GIF (*Graphic Interchange Format*) format is usually best suited for graphics that have mainly flat colors.

Tip: Use the 'ALT' tag when you use graphics on your Web site. The 'ALT' tag will display a text alternative for the visually impaired or users that have a text-only Web browser.

Rule #15: When in Doubt—Apply the "KIS" Rule

This rule is simple. If you are spending too much time pondering over using one graphic image versus another, or haggling over selecting a particular background color of a table, then "KIS." A common principle used by designers, "KIS" is an acronym that stands for "Keep It Simple."

When faced with making a decision (and when it comes to Web design, there are many), always go with the choice that is simplest. If, for instance, you are debating over whether or not to change the color of text from the default of black to a different color, keep the text black.

Rule #16: Guidelines for Working with Web Site Colors

Follow these guidelines when working with the color scheme on a Web site:

• Use a maximum of two or three colors throughout your Web site. One color should be the dominant color and the other an accent color. To illustrate this, think of the color scheme used to paint a house. The body of the house is usually painted one color (the dominant color), the trim or window shutters are usually painted a different color (the accent color). The same philosophy should be applied to your Web site's color scheme.

• Create a color scheme that coordinates with your Web site's overall message. What colors would you pick if you were asked to design a Web site for a company that sells cotton candy? The colors pink and white come to mind to reflect the color of cotton candy and the white cone used to hold it.

WEB DESIGN RULES

- Avoid using colors that make text difficult to read. Dark-colored text on a light-colored background is easier to read than light-colored text on a dark-colored background.
- Remember your R G B's. The different colors you see displayed on a Web page are made by mixing three colors: red, green, and blue. These color mixes are commonly referred to as RGB. Since you will be required to choose a predesigned Ultimate Fitness logo in your Web site, the RGB colors used to make the logo are provided for you in the simulation. You should use these colors throughout your Ultimate Fitness Web site.

Rule #17: Most Importantly—Have a Paper Plan

One of the worst habits you can develop as a Web site designer is to start building your Web site without first planning its design on paper. It is much easier to develop different design concepts and layout schemes on paper than it is on the computer.

Use a Web page planning form similar to the one provided on the Ultimate Fitness Resource CD to plan each Web page.

Use the Web Page Planning Form provided on the Ultimate Fitness Resource CD to plan and lay out each page of your Web site before beginning to work on the computer.

WEB DESIGN RULES

ULTIMATE FITNESS

Section 6:
The Individual Parts
of the Simulation

INCLUDED IN THIS SECTION:

Part 1:
Getting Started by
Planning and Organizing
Your Web Site

Approximate completion time for this section: 1-2 hours

This part of the simulation is divided into the following two sub-parts:

Part 1-A: Choose and Plan Your Web Site Navigation Structure on Paper
Part 1-B: Setting Up and Organizing Your Web Site on the Computer

Part 1-A: Choose and Plan Your Web Site Navigation Structure on Paper

TASK AND PURPOSE:

- To choose a navigation structure format to use in building the Ultimate Fitness Web site. For the Ultimate Fitness Web site, you are required to choose from one of two navigation structure formats. This is explained and illustrated in Step 2 of this part of the simulation.
- To create a paper sketch layout of the Ultimate Fitness Web site.

What is a navigation structure?

A Web site's navigation structure (also referred to as **shared borders**) are the parts of a Web site that are visible to users at all times. The navigation areas of a Web site usually include a logo, a slogan or tag-line, contact information, and navigation buttons that allow users to click into each main page within the Web site. The illustration below shows the two navigation formats available for use throughout the simulation.

Two Navigation Structure Formats Illustrated

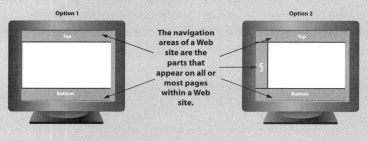

STRATEGIES AND DESIGN TIPS TO CONSIDER:

- Use graph paper when creating the paper sketch of your Web site navigation structure.
- When creating your paper sketch, use colored markers or pencils to help you differentiate between the different required elements and information of the navigation areas.
- Keep in mind that your paper sketch will serve as a guide only. The design of your Web site will be a work-in-progress.
- When preparing your paper sketch, consider the pixel width and height of your Web site. You don't want users to have to scroll to the right or too far down on your Web pages.
- To get some design inspiration for your paper sketch, use an Internet search engine and visit several health and fitness Web sites.

INSTRUCTIONS, INFORMATION, AND REQUIRED CONTENT:

NOTE: Read all the steps in this section before proceeding to Step 1 below.

Step 1:   Review the Ultimate Fitness Web site navigation flowchart.

Figure 1.1 illustrates the hierarchical organizational chart of the Ultimate Fitness Web site. You will use this chart as a guide in this section to plan and design your Ultimate Fitness Web site on paper. Becoming familiar with the structure and organization of the Web site will allow you to start mentally visualizing what your Web site will look like.

Review the chart in Figure 1.1 now.

Figure 1.1

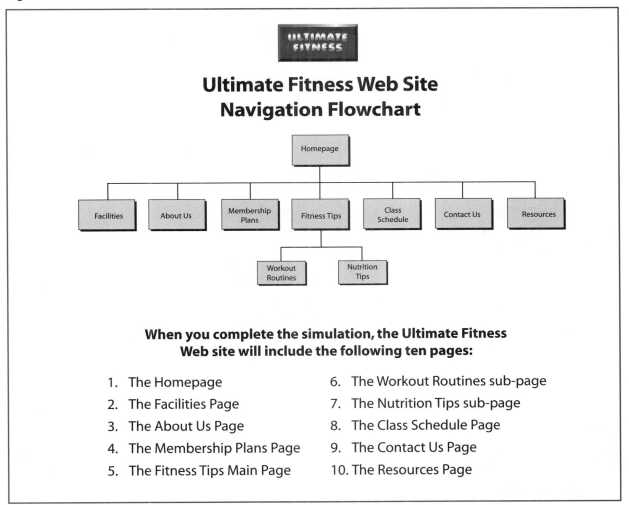

Ultimate Fitness Web Site Navigation Flowchart

When you complete the simulation, the Ultimate Fitness Web site will include the following ten pages:

1. The Homepage
2. The Facilities Page
3. The About Us Page
4. The Membership Plans Page
5. The Fitness Tips Main Page

6. The Workout Routines sub-page
7. The Nutrition Tips sub-page
8. The Class Schedule Page
9. The Contact Us Page
10. The Resources Page

Step 2:   Choose Your Web site's navigation structure format.

Before you can start sketching what your Web site will look like on paper, it is necessary to select a Web site navigation structure format to use throughout the remainder of the simulation. Remember, the information and content included within a Web site's navigation structure usually appears on all or most of the pages within a Web site. In the Ultimate Fitness Web site, the navigation areas will appear on every page.

While most of the design and layout of the Ultimate Fitness Web site will be left up to you, you are required to choose from one of the two navigation structure formats shown in Figure 1.2. Figure 1.2 also illustrates where the required content and information will be housed in the Ultimate Fitness Web site in each navigation area.

Do the following:

Review Figure 1.2 (shown on page 39) and then select one of the two Web site navigation structure formats shown below to use throughout the remainder of the simulation.

IMPORTANT STEP

Carefully review Figure 1.2 before selecting your Web site's navigation structure format.

Option 1: Top and Bottom Navigation Structure

Option 2: Top, Bottom, and Left Navigation Structure

Review Figure 1.2 (shown on page 39) and then select one of these two navigation structure formats to use throughout the simulation.

Figure 1.2

The Two Navigation Structure Format Options for the Ultimate Fitness Web Site

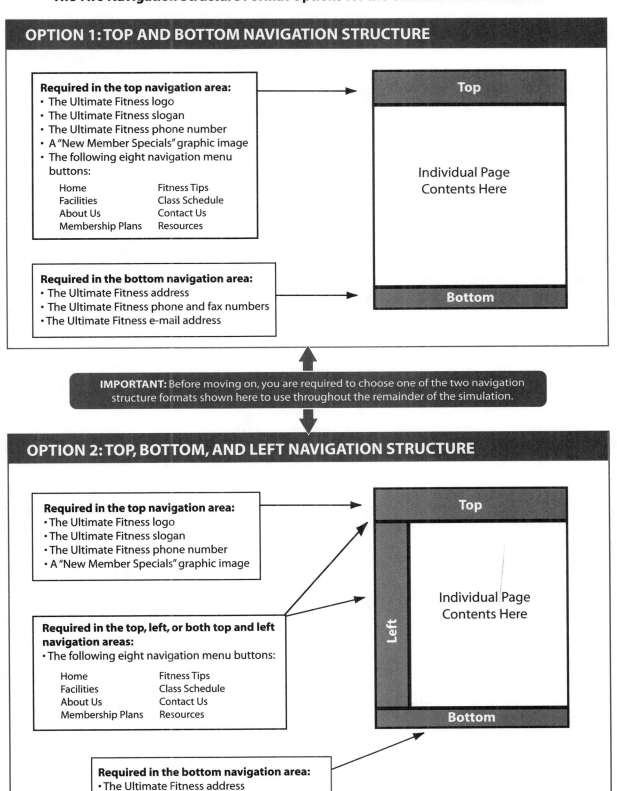

OPTION 1: TOP AND BOTTOM NAVIGATION STRUCTURE

Required in the top navigation area:
- The Ultimate Fitness logo
- The Ultimate Fitness slogan
- The Ultimate Fitness phone number
- A "New Member Specials" graphic image
- The following eight navigation menu buttons:

Home	Fitness Tips
Facilities	Class Schedule
About Us	Contact Us
Membership Plans	Resources

Required in the bottom navigation area:
- The Ultimate Fitness address
- The Ultimate Fitness phone and fax numbers
- The Ultimate Fitness e-mail address

Top

Individual Page Contents Here

Bottom

IMPORTANT: Before moving on, you are required to choose one of the two navigation structure formats shown here to use throughout the remainder of the simulation.

OPTION 2: TOP, BOTTOM, AND LEFT NAVIGATION STRUCTURE

Required in the top navigation area:
- The Ultimate Fitness logo
- The Ultimate Fitness slogan
- The Ultimate Fitness phone number
- A "New Member Specials" graphic image

Required in the top, left, or both top and left navigation areas:
- The following eight navigation menu buttons:

Home	Fitness Tips
Facilities	Class Schedule
About Us	Contact Us
Membership Plans	Resources

Required in the bottom navigation area:
- The Ultimate Fitness address
- The Ultimate Fitness phone and fax numbers
- The Ultimate Fitness e-mail address

Top

Left

Individual Page Contents Here

Bottom

Step 3: Choose an Ultimate Fitness Logo Style.

The next step to developing a paper sketch of your navigation structure will be to select an Ultimate Fitness logo style. While most of the design and layout decisions of the Ultimate Fitness Web site will be your own, the logo design styles you can use in your Web site have already been created and are available on the Ultimate Fitness Resource CD. *If you have not done so already, install the contents of the Ultimate Fitness Resource CD on your computer's hard drive at this time.*

There are a total of 32 different logo styles for you to choose from. Some sample logo styles are shown in Figure 1.3. All of the Ultimate Fitness logo files are in JPEG format and come in two sizes—large and small.

> The Ultimate Fitness logo styles can be found in the following directory:
>
> ***<drive letter>:\Ultimate Fitness Resource CD\Logos***

Take some time right now to explore the logo styles and select one to use throughout the simulation. Reviewing the logos will also give you an idea of what color schemes you can use in your Web site. The color scheme will be discussed in more detail in Part 1-B.

> **NOTE:** Because Ultimate Fitness is already an established business, you may not change, alter, or create your own logo. You must choose one logo from the available styles on the Ultimate Fitness Resource CD.

Figure 1.3

Ultimate Fitness Logo Style Samples

Before you plan your Web site's navigation structure on paper, select one of the logo styles provided on the Ultimate Fitness Resource CD. There are 32 styles to choose from.

The logo styles are in JPEG format and come in two different sizes—large and small.

The logos are installed in the following directory:

<drive letter>:\Ultimate Fitness Resource CD\Logos

DESIGN TIP

Select a logo style that matches the design theme you are mentally visualizing at this point in the simulation.

RESOURCE CD

The Ultimate Fitness logos are installed in the following directory:

<drive letter>:\Ultimate Fitness Resource CD\Logos

Step 4:   Plan, design, and lay out your Web site's navigation structure on paper.

Now that you have selected your Web site's navigation structure, selected an Ultimate Fitness logo style, and reviewed the required elements and information to be housed in the navigation areas of the Web site, it is time to create a paper sketch of your Web site's navigation structure.

It is important to have a plan on paper before you begin conducting any work with your Web site design software. It is equally important to remember that your paper sketch is only a rough draft of the Web site navigation structure and can be modified as you proceed with the development of your Web site.

Review Figure 1.2 once again and then lay out your Web site navigation structure on paper. Graph paper is especially helpful since most Web sites are built and designed using horizontal and vertical pattern schemes.

Figures 1.4 and 1.5 provide you with two sample paper sketches showing each of the two navigation structure formats you can choose from for use in the Ultimate Fitness simulation.

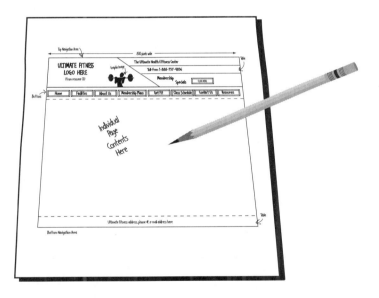

DESIGN TIP

Use graph paper to create the paper sketch of the navigation structure of your Web site.

RESOURCE CD

Before creating your paper sketch, browse the fitness images provided on the Ultimate Fitness Resource CD to get some design inspiration.

The fitness images are installed in the following directory:

<drive letter>:\Ultimate Fitness Resource CD\ Fitness Images

DESIGN TIP

Remember that your paper sketch is just a starting point. The final design of your Web site will probably look a bit different when complete.

✓ CHECK POINT

The paper sketch of your navigation structure should be complete before moving on to the next part of the simulation.

Figure 1.4: Sample Paper Sketch of a Top and Bottom Navigation Structure Format

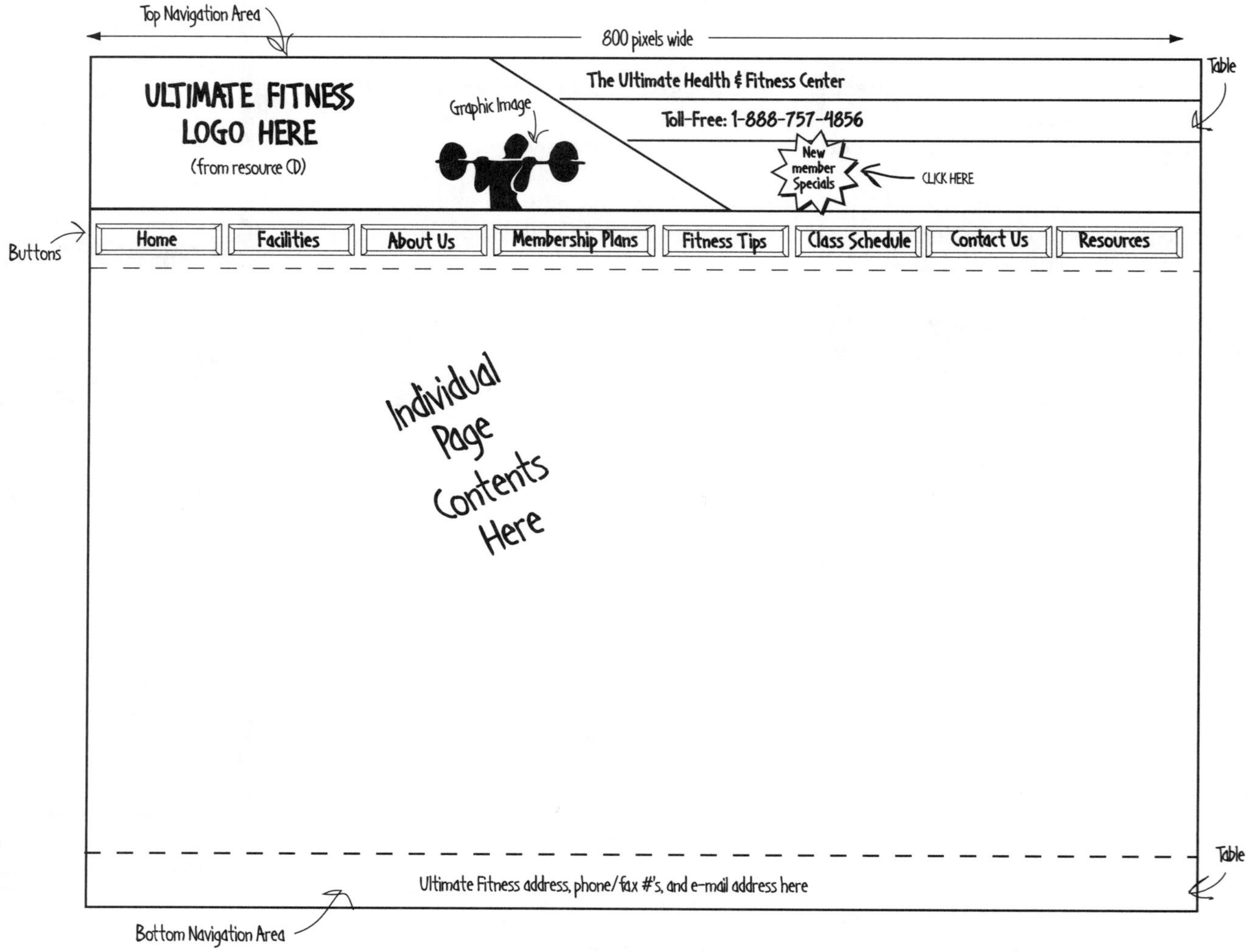

Top Navigation Area

800 pixels wide

Table

ULTIMATE FITNESS LOGO HERE

(from resource CD)

Graphic Image

The Ultimate Health & Fitness Center

Toll-Free: 1-888-757-4856

New member Specials

CLICK HERE

Buttons

| Home | Facilities | About Us | Membership Plans | Fitness Tips | Class Schedule | Contact Us | Resources |

Individual Page Contents Here

Table

Ultimate Fitness address, phone/fax #'s, and e-mail address here

Bottom Navigation Area

Figure 1.5: Sample Paper Sketch of a Top, Left, and Bottom Navigation Structure Format

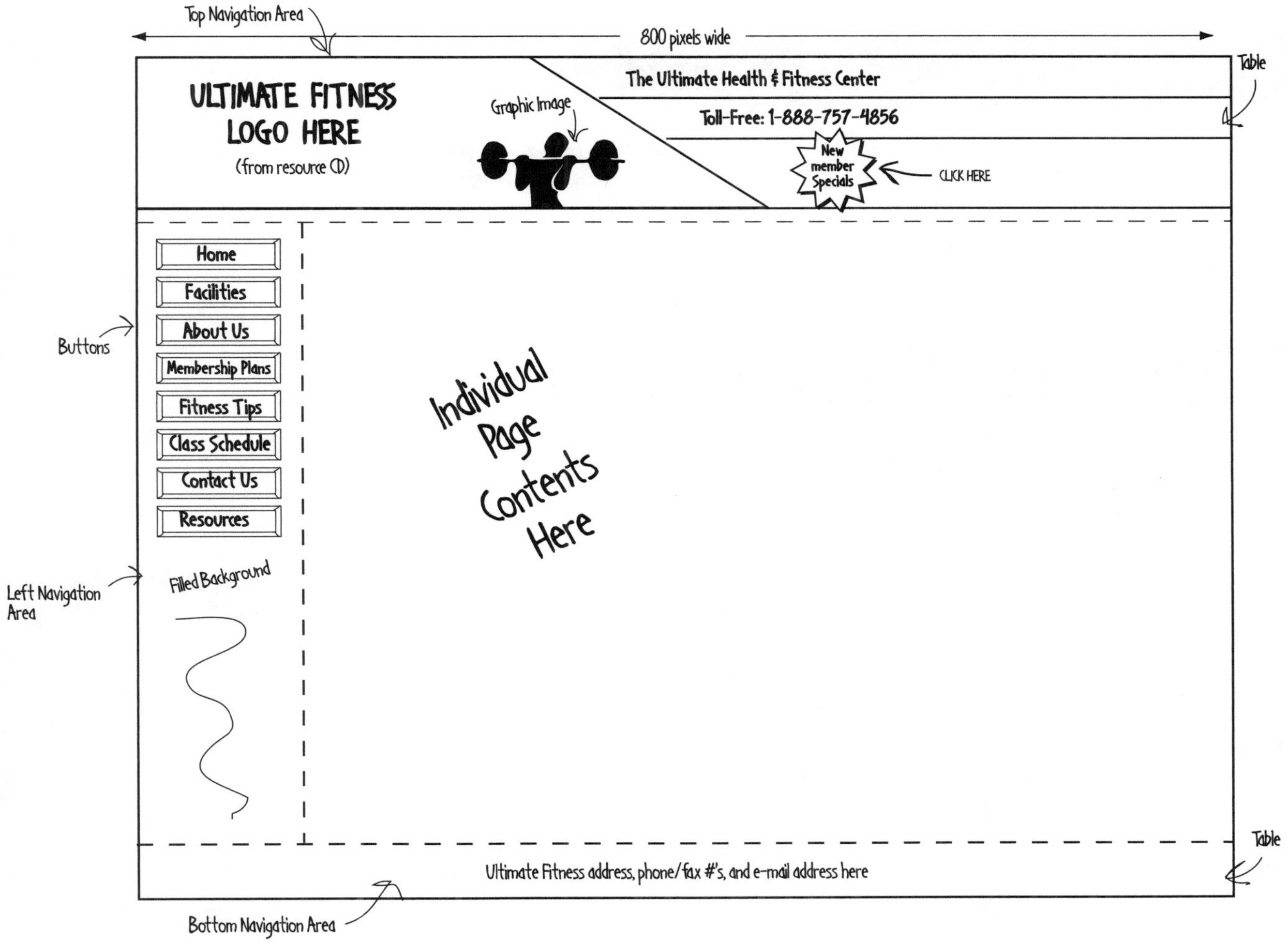

Top Navigation Area

800 pixels wide

Table

ULTIMATE FITNESS LOGO HERE
(from resource CD)

Graphic Image

The Ultimate Health & Fitness Center

Toll-Free: 1-888-757-4856

New member Specials

CLICK HERE

Buttons

Home
Facilities
About Us
Membership Plans
Fitness Tips
Class Schedule
Contact Us
Resources

Individual Page Contents Here

Left Navigation Area

Filled Background

Table

Ultimate Fitness address, phone/fax #'s, and e-mail address here

Bottom Navigation Area

Part 1-B: Setting Up and Organizing Your Web Site on the Computer

TASK AND PURPOSE:

Now that you have selected and planned your Web site's navigation structure on paper, it is time to begin using your Web site design software to build the Ultimate Fitness Web site. In this part of the simulation, you will use your Web site design software to create a new Web site and set up folders on your hard drive that will help you organize the Web images and files you will be using throughout the simulation.

INSTRUCTIONS, INFORMATION, AND REQUIRED CONTENT:

NOTE: Read all the steps in this section before proceeding to Step 1 below.

Step 1:   Create a new folder and name it *Ultimate_Fitness*.

On your computer's hard drive, create a new folder and name it *Ultimate_Fitness* (see Figure 1.6). All of your Ultimate Fitness Web site files will be stored in this folder.

Step 2:   Set up your Ultimate Fitness Web site.

Using your Web site design software, start a new Web site and name it *Ultimate_Fitness* (see Figure 1.6). Be sure that you specify that the files for your new Web site be stored in the *Ultimate_Fitness* folder you created in Step 1.

If you are required at this time to specify a Web site format, be sure that the format of the Web site matches the navigation structure you selected in Part 1-A. Otherwise, this procedure will be covered in Step 4 of this part of the simulation.

> **IMPORTANT STEP**
>
> Be sure that you set up your Web site to store all files in a folder titled *Ultimate_Fitness*.

> **Note:** Check with your instructor to see if your Web site should be set up under a specific folder on your computer or computer network system. If this is the case, you will need to substitute the folders referenced in the simulation with the designated folders you set up.

Step 3:   Create image folders to help you stay organized.

Since you will be working with a large number of Web images throughout this simulation, it will be important to save your files in folders that make them easy to access and organize.

Do the following:

1. Create a folder within the *Ultimate_Fitness* Web site folder you created in Step 1 (*Ultimate_Fitness*) and name it *UF_Images* (see Figure 1.6).

   This folder will be used to store and save all graphic images that you use in your Ultimate Fitness Web site.

2. Create a second folder within the *Ultimate_Fitness* Web site folder you created in Step 1 (*Ultimate_Fitness*) and name it *UF_Buttons* (see Figure 1.6).

   This folder will be used to store and save the navigation menu buttons you will create in Part 2 of the simulation.

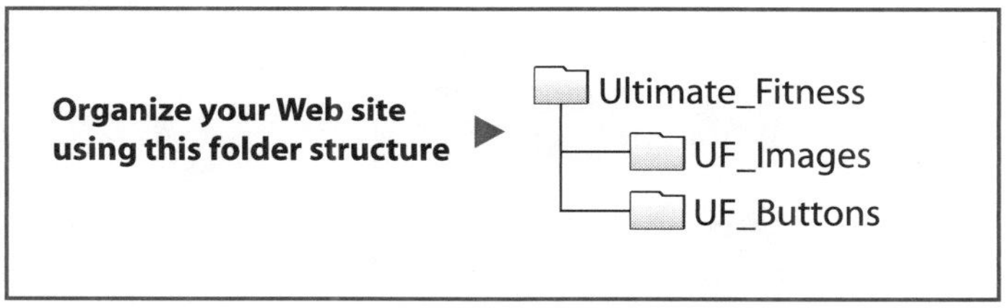

DESIGN TIP

Every good Web designer keeps his files organized by creating and naming folders. This makes it easy to access, find, and edit files as each Web page of a Web site is completed.

Figure 1.6

Organize your Web site using this folder structure ▶

📁 Ultimate_Fitness
    📁 UF_Images
    📁 UF_Buttons

Step 4: **Define your Web site's navigation structure format using your Web site design software.**

With the Ultimate Fitness Web site open, set up the Web site to display the shared navigation areas based on the navigation structure format you selected in Part 1-A. *You must set up your Web site so that the navigation areas will appear on every page in your Ultimate Fitness Web site (see Figure 1.7).*

Consult with your Web design software and/or your instructor to see how to define the shared navigation areas based on the navigation structure format you have selected.

Note: Defining shared navigation areas can differ based on the Web design software application you are using. Some Web design software applications require the user to define shared borders which will serve as the shared navigation areas, while others allow users to define the Web site's shared navigation areas as a template.

IMPORTANT STEP

You must set up your Web site so that the navigation areas appear on every page of your Web site.

Figure 1.7

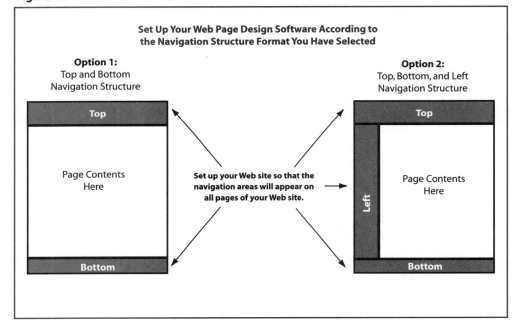

Step 5: Save the shared navigation areas of your Web site as *"UF_template."*

With this step complete, you are now ready to begin building the individual shared navigation areas of your Ultimate Fitness Web site, which you will do in the next part of the simulation.

WEB FACT

Web file names containing more than two words are usually separated by underscores (_). This is because Web browsers do not recognize spaces as characters. @

Before moving on to the next part of the simulation, the shared navigation areas of your Web site should be set up and saved properly using your Web site design software.

Part 2:
Design and Build the
Shared Navigation Areas

Approximate completion time for this section: 4-6 hours

This part of the simulation is divided into the following three sub-parts:

Part 2-A: Design and Build the Top Shared Navigation Area
Part 2-B: Design, Build, and Add Navigation Menu Buttons to the Top and/or Left Shared Navigation Area(s)
Part 2-C: Design and Build the Bottom Shared Navigation Area

Part 2-A: Design and Build the Top Shared Navigation Area

WEB FACT

The top navigation area of a Web site gets the highest visibility from Web site visitors. Take your time designing your top navigation area.

@

TASK AND PURPOSE:

- To design and build the top shared navigation area of the Ultimate Fitness Web site.

  In this part of the simulation, you will be adding the following elements and information to the top shared navigation area of the Ultimate Fitness Web site (see Figure 2.1):

  - The Ultimate Fitness logo
  - The Ultimate Fitness slogan
  - The Ultimate Fitness phone number
  - A "New Member Specials" button, starburst, or callout graphic image

Figure 2.1

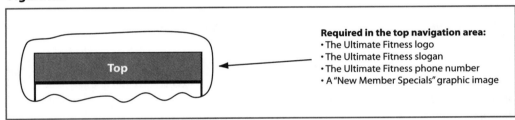

Top

Required in the top navigation area:
- The Ultimate Fitness logo
- The Ultimate Fitness slogan
- The Ultimate Fitness phone number
- A "New Member Specials" graphic image

STRATEGIES AND DESIGN TIPS TO CONSIDER:

- Use the paper sketch you created in Part 1 as a guide when developing the top shared navigation area on the computer.
- The top shared navigation area of any Web site will get the most visibility; therefore, pay careful attention to its design.
- Pay attention to the pixel width of any tables that you use to create the top shared navigation area. A safe pixel width to use is 800 pixels or less. This will allow the entire width of your Web site to properly display on most monitors. Web site visitors will not have to scroll to the right to view the site.

DESIGN TIP

Use the paper sketch you created in Part 1 as a guide as you design and build your top shared navigation area.

INSTRUCTIONS, INFORMATION, AND REQUIRED CONTENT:

NOTE: Read all of the steps in this section before proceeding to Step 1 below.

Step 1: **With the Ultimate Fitness Web site open, open the file "*UF_template*" that you created in Part 1-B.**

Step 2: **Insert your selected Ultimate Fitness logo style into the top shared navigation area of the page.**

Insert the Ultimate Fitness logo that you selected in Part 1-A into the top shared navigation area of your Web site.

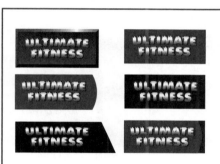

Insert the Ultimate Fitness logo that you selected in Part 1-A, Step 3 into the top shared navigation area of your Web site.

The logos are installed in the following directory from the Ultimate Fitness Resource CD:

<drive letter>:\Ultimate Fitness Resource CD\Logos

Step 3: **Establish a Web site color scheme.**

To stay consistent with the Ultimate Fitness health and fitness color scheme, your Web site must include the colors that were used in the Ultimate Fitness logo style you have selected. Every Web site design software comes equipped with a feature that allows users to define custom colors.

Depending on the Web site design software you are using, defining custom colors is achieved using one of the two methods described below.

Methods to define custom colors using Web site design software:

Method 1: RGB (Red, Green, and Blue)
This method allows users to define custom colors by changing the red, green, and blue color mix, commonly referred to as RGB.

Method 2: Hexadecimal Value
This method allows users to define custom colors by changing the hexadecimal value.

If you look at the Ultimate Fitness logo styles installed from the Ultimate Fitness Resource CD, you will notice that most of them include a consistent color scheme. The majority of the logo styles contain a mix of the colors blue, grey, black, and white.

Tables 2.1 and 2.2 provide the color chart mixtures for both the RGB and hexadecimal methods of defining custom colors that will match the colors used to create the Ultimate Fitness logo. These colors should be used in your Ultimate Fitness Web site to establish a consistent, professional color scheme. Consider using these colors in the production of graphics, buttons, tables, and text throughout the simulation. ***Be careful not to overdo it. When it comes to colors, less is better than more.***

Note: For easy reference, the Ultimate Fitness Web Color Charts are shown in the right-margin areas throughout this simulation.

Color Charts to Define Custom Colors in Your Web Site

Check with your Web site design software to see which method (either RGB or Hexadecimal) to use to define custom colors that match the Ultimate Fitness logo styles.

Table 2.1

Ultimate Fitness RGB Web Color Chart				
Color	Blue	Black	Grey	White
Red (R)	18	0	102	255
Green (G)	52	0	102	255
Blue (B)	90	0	102	255

Table 2.2

Ultimate Fitness Hexadecimal Values Web Color Chart	
Color	Hexadecimal Values
Blue	Hex={12, 34, 5A}
Black	Hex={00, 00, 00}
Grey	Hex={66, 66, 66}
White	Hex={FF, FF, FF}

The color charts shown in Tables 2.1 and 2.2 can be viewed and printed from the Ultimate Fitness Resource CD. The file is titled "*Color Charts*" and is located in the following directory:

<drive letter>:\Ultimate Fitness Resource CD\Student Documents

---

DESIGN TIP

Experiment with using background colors in the top shared navigation menu. Use the color charts provided to match the Ultimate Fitness logo style you have selected.

DESIGN TIP

Use a maximum base of 2-3 colors throughout your Web site. Too many colors will give your Web site a confusing, unprofessional look and feel.

IMPORTANT STEP

Use the color charts to create a color scheme in your Web site that matches the colors used to create the Ultimate Fitness logos.

Step 4: **Add the Ultimate Fitness slogan shown below to the top shared navigation area.**

"The Ultimate Fitness and Health Center"

You can either use the text tool within your Web site design software or create a Web graphic image of the slogan using a Web graphic design software application.

Step 5: **Add the Ultimate Fitness phone number shown below to the top shared navigation area.**

1.888.757.4856

Step 6: **Create a "New Member Specials" button, starburst, or callout graphic to add to the top shared navigation area.**

Ultimate Fitness often runs promotional specials to attract new members to its fitness center. To encourage new members to read about the new member specials, you will create a clickable graphic image that highlights the new member specials on the Ultimate Fitness Web site. This new member specials graphic image will be hyperlinked to the membership plans page later in the simulation.

An example of what this graphic might look like when designed is shown in Figure 2.2. You may add additional text to the graphic image.

Create the graphic image using your Web graphic design software. **Save the graphic image as "*new_specials*" to the *UF_Images* folder.**

Figure 2.2

Example of a New Member Specials graphic image to be inserted into the top shared navigation area of your Web site.

Step 7: **Insert the "New Member Specials" graphic image (file name "*new_specials*" created in Step 6 to the top shared navigation area.**

DESIGN TIP

When entering text in your Web site, use the following Web-safe fonts so that they will display correctly when viewed in an Internet browser:

- Arial
- Courier
- Georgia
- Helvetica
- Times New Roman
- Verdana

DESIGN TIP

Be sure to keep the size, style, and color of the text you enter consistent with the style and design theme you have established for your Web site.

QUICK REFERENCE COLOR CHARTS

Ultimate Fitness RGB Web Color Chart				
Color	Blue	Black	Grey	White
Red (R)	18	0	102	255
Green (G)	52	0	102	255
Blue (B)	90	0	102	255

Ultimate Fitness Hexadecimal Values Web Color Chart	
Color	Hexadecimal Values
Blue	Hex={12, 34, 5A}
Black	Hex={00, 00, 00}
Grey	Hex={66, 66, 66}
White	Hex={FF, FF, FF}

Step 8: **Add additional text and/or graphic images to the top shared navigation area.**

You may add additional text and/or graphic images that will help enhance the look and appearance of the top shared navigation area. Consider using a fitness-related image for a background. You may use one or more of the fitness images installed from the Ultimate Fitness Resource CD located in the following directory:

<drive letter>:\Ultimate Fitness Resource CD\Fitness Images

Save any graphic images that you add to the *UF_Images* folder.

Step 9: **Save the file before moving on to the next part of the simulation.**

✓ CHECK POINT

Carefully review all the steps included in this section to ensure you have included all the required elements and information in your top shared navigation area. Preview the Web site using your Internet browser and make any necessary changes before moving on to the next part of the simulation.

DESIGN TIP

When adding additional text or graphic images, be careful not to overcrowd the top shared navigation area of your Web site.

RESOURCE CD

Consider using one or more of the fitness images available from the Ultimate Fitness Resource CD to enhance your Web site. The fitness images are installed in the following directory:

<drive letter>:\Ultimate Fitness Resource CD\ Fitness Images

QUICK REFERENCE COLOR CHARTS

Ultimate Fitness RGB Web Color Chart				
Color	Blue	Black	Grey	White
Red (R)	18	0	102	255
Green (G)	52	0	102	255
Blue (B)	90	0	102	255

Ultimate Fitness Hexadecimal Values Web Color Chart	
Color	Hexadecimal Values
Blue	Hex={12, 34, 5A}
Black	Hex={00, 00, 00}
Grey	Hex={66, 66, 66}
White	Hex={FF, FF, FF}

Part 2-B: Design, Build, and Add Navigation Menu Buttons to the Top and/or Left Shared Navigation Area(s)

TASK AND PURPOSE:

• To design each of the eight required navigation menu buttons and add them to either the top, left, or both the top and left shared navigation area(s). The navigation menu buttons will allow Web site visitors to go to each page in the Ultimate Fitness Web site.

Where you place the navigation menu buttons will depend on which navigation structure format you have selected to use from Part 1-A (see Figure 2.3).

Figure 2.3

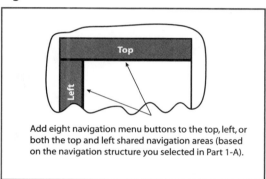

Add eight navigation menu buttons to the top, left, or both the top and left shared navigation areas (based on the navigation structure you selected in Part 1-A).

STRATEGIES AND DESIGN TIPS TO CONSIDER:

• Keep the size of the buttons relatively the same to create a consistent, clean, and professional look.
• Carefully plan the pixel height and width of your buttons so that they will fit proportionately and symmetrically in your chosen shared navigation area.
• Use the same font style and color scheme when designing your menu buttons. This will help to maintain a consistent look and feel throughout the Web site.
• Consider using a *rollover* effect when designing your menu buttons (sometimes referred to as *swap* or *hover* buttons). Using this effect will make your menu buttons interactive and appear to be "pushed in" when users navigate through your Web site.

DESIGN TIP

Consider using a button *rollover* effect when creating your navigation menu buttons. This effect is also sometimes referred to as a *swap* or *hover* button effect.

The rollover effect is commonly applied to Web site buttons so that when users move the mouse pointer over each button, it changes color, glows, or gives a "pushed-in" appearance. Applying this effect will make the menu buttons interactive for the user.

To do this, you will need to build two or three versions of each button.

DESIGN TIP

The color of your buttons should complement or match the colors used in the Ultimate Fitness logo style you have selected to use in your Web site.

INSTRUCTIONS, INFORMATION, AND REQUIRED CONTENT:

NOTE: Read all of the steps in this section before proceeding to Step 1 below.

Step 1:   Design and build the required navigation menu buttons.

Using your Web graphic design software, you will design and build the required eight navigation menu buttons for the Ultimate Fitness Web site.

> **Note**: If you selected a top and bottom navigation structure, you will place all eight buttons horizontally across the top navigation area. If you selected a top, left, and bottom navigation structure, you can place all eight buttons across the top horizontally, in the left navigation area vertically, or you can divide the buttons by placing some in the top and some in the left shared navigation areas. Follow your paper sketch as a guide.

Table 2.3 provides the required eight navigation menu buttons that must be designed and placed in the Ultimate Fitness Web site shared navigation area(s). A description of the page that corresponds with each button is also provided in Table 2.3.

> ***Do the following:***

Review the information provided in Table 2.3. Then, design and build each of the eight navigation menu buttons using your Web graphic design software. **Save each button in the UF_Buttons folder using the file names given in Table 2.3.**

Step 2:   With the Ultimate Fitness Web site open, open the file "UF_template."

Step 3:   Based on the navigation structure you selected in Part 1, insert the required navigation menu buttons in either the top, left, or both the top and left navigation areas (see Figure 2.4).

Figure 2.4

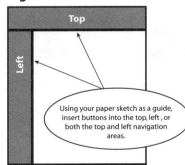

Using your paper sketch as a guide, insert buttons into the top, left , or both the top and left navigation areas.

> **Note**: You will hyperlink each of the navigation buttons to their corresponding pages as each page is built throughout the simulation.

DESIGN TIP

Keep the size of your menu buttons relatively the same to create a consistent, clean, professional look throughout your Web site.

IMPORTANT STEP

Be sure to save each menu button using the file names provided in Table 2.3. Save each menu button to the UF_Buttons folder.

QUICK REFERENCE COLOR CHARTS

Ultimate Fitness RGB Web Color Chart				
Color	Blue	Black	Grey	White
Red (R)	18	0	102	255
Green (G)	52	0	102	255
Blue (B)	90	0	102	255

Ultimate Fitness Hexadecimal Values Web Color Chart	
Color	Hexadecimal Values
Blue	Hex={12, 34, 5A}
Black	Hex={00, 00, 00}
Grey	Hex={66, 66, 66}
White	Hex={FF, FF, FF}

Table 2.3

Required Navigation Menu Buttons in the Ultimate Fitness Web Site		
Button Title	Description of corresponding page	Save As File Name
Home	The *Homepage* will be the first page Web site visitors will see. The home button will allow visitors to return to the homepage when browsing through the Web site.	Home
Facilities	The *Facilities* page will provide Web site visitors with an overview of the Ultimate Fitness facility including a description of the free weight, cardio, and aerobic fitness rooms.	Facilities
About Us	The *About Us* page will give Web site visitors a description and background of the Ultimate Fitness establishment.	About_Us
Membership Plans	The *Membership Plans* page will provide Web site visitors with information on how to join Ultimate Fitness including various membership plans, prices, and specials.	Member_Plans
Fitness Tips	The *Fitness Tips* page will provide Web site visitors with a variety of workout routines, nutritional information and tips, and describe the personal training program available to Ultimate Fitness members.	Fitness_Tips
Class Schedule	The *Class Schedule* page will provide existing Ultimate Fitness members with current news, updates, and events happening at the Ultimate Fitness establishment.	Class_Schedule
Contact Us	The *Contact Us* page will provide Web site visitors with contact information including the Ultimate Fitness address, e-mail address, phone and fax numbers, and the hours of operation.	Contact_Us
Resources	The *Resources* page will give Web site visitors links to popular health and fitness-related Web sites.	Resources

Step 4: **Add alternate text to each navigation menu button.**

Add the alternate text shown in Table 2.4 to each of the corresponding navigation menu buttons.

What is alternate text?
   Alternate Text (ALT text) is short phrases of text that become visible when the user hovers his or her mouse pointer over a button or graphic. Alternate text helps users find out more about Web site pages without actually clicking the button or graphic link. An example is shown below:

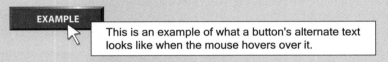

EXAMPLE

This is an example of what a button's alternate text looks like when the mouse hovers over it.

Note: If necessary, consult with your Web site design software and/or instructor to learn how to add alternate text to your menu buttons.

Table 2.4

| Alternate Text Required for Each Navigation Menu Button ||
Button Title	Alternate Text
Home	*Ultimate Fitness homepage*
Facilities	*Learn more about the Ultimate Fitness facilities*
About Us	*Read more about Ultimate Fitness*
Membership Plans	*Learn how to join, view membership plans, pricing, and specials*
Fitness Tips	*Workout routines, nutrition tips, and more*
Class Schedule	*Ultimate Fitness news, events, and updates*
Contact Us	*How to reach Ultimate Fitness*
Resources	*Visit popular health and fitness-related Web sites*

Step 5: **If you have elected to use a left shared navigation area, you may add additional text and/or graphic images to it now.**

Save any graphic images that you add to the *UF_Images* folder.

Step 6: **Save the file.**

✓ CHECK POINT

Carefully review all the steps provided in this section to ensure you have designed and inserted all eight required navigation menu buttons in your top and/or left shared navigation area(s). Preview the Web site using your Internet browser and make any necessary changes before moving on to the next part of the simulation.

DESIGN TIP

If you are placing some or all of the menu buttons in the left navigation area, be sure to keep the width of each button identical. Doing so will allow you to neatly stack the buttons vertically, giving them a professionally designed look.

Part 2-C: Design and Build the Bottom Shared Navigation Area

TASK AND PURPOSE:

- To add the Ultimate Fitness contact information to the bottom navigation area of the Ultimate Fitness Web site (see Figure 2.5).
- To add a hyperlink to the Ultimate Fitness e-mail address.

Figure 2.5

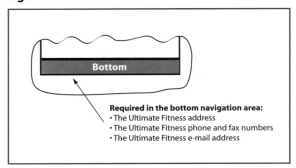

Bottom

Required in the bottom navigation area:
- The Ultimate Fitness address
- The Ultimate Fitness phone and fax numbers
- The Ultimate Fitness e-mail address

STRATEGIES AND DESIGN TIPS TO CONSIDER:

- Since the bottom of any Web site is usually the least visible, use plain, easy-to-read text.
- Use a table that is the same pixel width as the one used to create your top shared navigation area.
- Use a background color or colors similar to or identical to those that you used in the top navigation area or a color used in the buttons you created.
- Consider aligning the text to the left or the center of the table in which you create the bottom navigation area.
- To save space, place the address, phone number, fax number, and e-mail address side-by-side separating each with a bullet symbol.
- Since this will be the first time you hyperlink text, experiment with different hyperlink effects. *Do you want the text to be underlined when hyperlinked? What color do you want the text to be once the Web site visitor has clicked on the hyperlinked text?*

INSTRUCTIONS, INFORMATION, AND REQUIRED CONTENT:

NOTE: Read all of the steps in this section before proceeding to Step 1 below.

Step 1:   **With the Ultimate Fitness Web site open, open the file "*UF_template*."**

Step 2:   **Add the following Ultimate Fitness contact information to the bottom shared navigation area:**

350 Park Avenue • New York, NY 10019
Phone: 1.888.757.4856 • Fax: 1.888.757.4987
E-mail: contact@uf-online.com

Step 3:   **Hyperlink the Ultimate Fitness e-mail address.**

Select the e-mail address you entered in Step 1 above and add a hyperlink that will send e-mail to the Ultimate Fitness e-mail address. Doing this will allow Web site visitors to e-mail Ultimate Fitness by clicking on the e-mail address hyperlink. The result should look similar to the one shown below.

E-mail: underline{contact@uf-online.com}

> **Note**: If necessary, consult with your Web site design software and/ or instructor to learn how to apply an e-mail hyperlink.

Step 4:   **Place the following text in the bottom navigation area:**

©*<insert current year here>*. Ultimate Fitness.
Web site design by *<insert your name here>*.

Step 5:   **Save the file.**

✓ CHECK POINT

Carefully review all the steps provided in this section to ensure you have included all the information required for the bottom shared navigation area. Preview the Web site using your Internet browser and make any necessary changes before moving on to the next part of the simulation.

DESIGN TIP

Keep the size, style, and color of the text you enter consistent with the style and design theme you have established for your Web site.

DESIGN TIP

Experiment with the way you want your hyperlinked text to appear. Keep your hyperlinked text style identical throughout your entire Web site.

QUICK REFERENCE COLOR CHARTS

Ultimate Fitness RGB Web Color Chart				
Color	Blue	Black	Grey	White
Red (R)	18	0	102	255
Green (G)	52	0	102	255
Blue (B)	90	0	102	255

Ultimate Fitness Hexadecimal Values Web Color Chart	
Color	Hexadecimal Values
Blue	Hex={12, 34, 5A}
Black	Hex={00, 00, 00}
Grey	Hex={66, 66, 66}
White	Hex={FF, FF, FF}

ULTIMATE FITNESS

Part 3:
Design and Build
the Homepage

Approximate completion time for this section: 2-3 hours

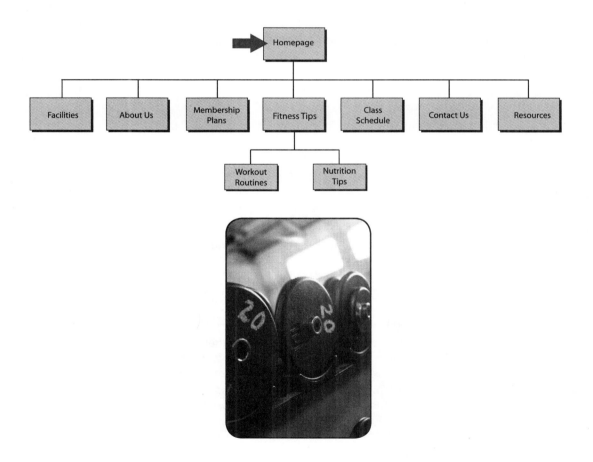

Part 3: Design and Build the Homepage

TASK AND PURPOSE:

- To design and build the Homepage for the Ultimate Fitness Web site.
- The purpose of the Homepage is to provide Web site visitors with an overview of the Ultimate Fitness establishment.

STRATEGIES AND DESIGN TIPS TO CONSIDER:

- The Homepage is the most visible and visited page of every Web site. It is the one page that will either keep visitors interested or turn them away to another Web site. Take your time when designing the homepage.
- Try to provide a friendly, welcoming layout and design on your Homepage.
- Keep your font selection consistent throughout not only the Homepage, but every page you create on the Web site. The same rule applies for applying colors and styles to text and graphic images.
- Whenever a substantial amount of text appears on a page, consider using graphic images to help visitors visualize the message being conveyed.
- Consider adding a picture caption to give meaning to any graphic image that you add to your Web site.
- Use colors that are consistent with those provided in the Ultimate Fitness Web Color Charts.
- Before you begin building the Homepage using your Web design software, read all of the instructions, information, and required content provided in this part of the simulation.
- Use the Web Page Planning form to create a thumbnail sketch of the layout and design of your Homepage.

Now is a good time to print several copies of the Web Page Planning Form installed from the Ultimate Fitness Resource CD. You will need one copy for each remaining part of the simulation. The Web Page Planning Form can be accessed and printed from the following directory:

<drive letter>:\Ultimate Fitness Resource CD\Student Documents

WEB FACT

The Homepage is the first page Web site visitors will see. It is the "first impression" a Web designer will make. Remember to take your time in planning your Homepage. You don't get a second chance to make a good first impression.

RESOURCE CD

Use the Web Page Planning Form installed from the Ultimate Fitness Resource CD to plan your Homepage on paper before starting any work on the computer.

INSTRUCTIONS, INFORMATION, AND REQUIRED CONTENT:

NOTE: Read all of the steps in this section before proceeding to Step 1 below.

Step 1: **With the Ultimate Fitness Web site open, do the following:**

1. Open the file *"UF_template."*
2. From the *File* menu of your software, choose *Save As* and rename the file *"index."*

Note: Before you begin this section, be sure that all of the navigation areas you have previously built and designed are visible in the work area within your Web site design software.

Step 2: **Add the following browser page title to the Homepage:**

Ultimate Fitness: The Ultimate Health and Fitness Center

What is a browser page title?
The browser page title is the text that you add to a Web page's properties so that it appears in a Web browser's title bar. An example is shown below.

Note: If necessary, consult with your Web site design software and/or instructor to learn how to add a browser page title to a Web page.

Step 3: **Add the following headline to the top area of the Homepage:**

Welcome to Ultimate Fitness:
The Ultimate Health and Fitness Center

Format the text so that it is consistent with the style and design theme you have established for your Web site.

Note: You may change the wording of the headline as long as it does not change its meaning or interpretation.

IMPORTANT STEP

Do not forget to add the browser page title to the Homepage.

DESIGN TIP

Keep the headline text in your homepage consistent with the style and design theme you have established for your Web site.

Step 4: Add the text given below beneath the headline you added in Step 3.

Format the text so that it is consistent with the style and design theme you have established for your Web site.

> Since 1998, Ultimate Fitness has provided the amenities of a large health club chain, with the service and personality of a hometown gym. Please browse our site to find out about our top-rated facility.
>
> Come check us out using our free one-week trial pass located on the "Membership Plans" page.
>
> Ultimate Fitness is a proud member of The International Health, Racquet & Sports Club Association (IHRSA). IHRSA is a non-profit trade association representing health & fitness facilities, gyms, spas, sports clubs, and suppliers worldwide. The Mission of IHRSA is to grow, protect, and promote the industry, and to provide its members with benefits that will help them be more successful.
>
> We have membership plans to meet any budget. For example, if working out and training on the weekend doesn't fit your schedule, Ultimate Fitness is proud to be one of the few fitness facilities offering weekday-only memberships.

Note: You will be required to hyperlink the text that reads "Membership Plans" above to the membership plans page, which you will create in Part 6 of the simulation.

Step 5: Add a graphic image to enhance the visual appeal of the text you entered in Step 4.

A variety of fitness-related images are installed from the Ultimate Fitness Resource CD located in the following directory:

<drive letter>:\Ultimate Fitness Resource CD\Fitness Images

Save any graphic images that you add to the *UF_Images* folder.

DESIGN TIP

Consider dividing the welcome message text into columns to make it easier to read for Web site visitors.

QUICK REFERENCE COLOR CHARTS

Ultimate Fitness RGB Web Color Chart

Color	Blue	Black	Grey	White
Red (R)	18	0	102	255
Green (G)	52	0	102	255
Blue (B)	90	0	102	255

Ultimate Fitness Hexadecimal Values Web Color Chart

Color	Hexadecimal Values
Blue	Hex={12, 34, 5A}
Black	Hex={00, 00, 00}
Grey	Hex={66, 66, 66}
White	Hex={FF, FF, FF}

RESOURCE CD

Consider using one of the fitness images available from the Ultimate Fitness Resource CD to enhance your Web site. The fitness images are installed in the following directory:

<drive letter>:\Ultimate Fitness Resource CD\ Fitness Images

Step 6: Create two VIP Member Passes as graphic images.

To help attract new members, Ultimate Fitness will include two VIP (*Very Important Person*) passes on its homepage. Both of these passes will be hyperlinked to the *Membership Plans* page later in the simulation.

Use your Web graphic design software to create the two VIP passes shown in Figure 3.1. Design the VIP passes so that they look professional and are consistent with the design theme you have established thus far. Experiment with adding graphic images and typefaces (fonts) that will be eye-catching to the visitor.

Save the VIP graphic images to the *UF_Images* folder as *"VIP1"* and *"VIP2,"* respectively.

Figure 3.1

> **VIP Pass Graphic Image #1:**
>
> > VIP PASS
> > 50% Off One-Month Membership!
> > Pay Only $17.99 for your first month. Just mention this Web site coupon when you call or come in to Ultimate Fitness.
>
> **VIP Pass Graphic Image #2:**
>
> > VIP PASS
> > Free One-Week Trial Pass!
> > Come in free for one week and try Ultimate Fitness. Just mention this Web site coupon when you call or visit Ultimate Fitness.

Note: You will hyperlink the two VIP graphics to the *Membership Plans* page after it is built later in the simulation.

Step 7: Place the two VIP Pass graphic images on the Homepage.

Insert the two VIP passes you created in Step 6 above on the Homepage. Be sure to place these images in an area on the Homepage where they will easily be seen by Web site visitors.

DESIGN TIP

When creating the two VIP graphic images, consider designing each one to look like a coupon. This will encourage users to click on the graphics.

DESIGN TIP

To help draw attention to the VIP passes, consider using a graphic image inside each of them.

QUICK REFERENCE COLOR CHARTS

Ultimate Fitness RGB Web Color Chart				
Color	Blue	Black	Grey	White
Red (R)	18	0	102	255
Green (G)	52	0	102	255
Blue (B)	90	0	102	255

Ultimate Fitness Hexadecimal Values Web Color Chart	
Color	Hexadecimal Values
Blue	Hex={12, 34, 5A}
Black	Hex={00, 00, 00}
Grey	Hex={66, 66, 66}
White	Hex={FF, FF, FF}

Step 8: Add the following headline to the Homepage:

Our Class Schedule is Now Online!

Format the text so that it is consistent with the style and design theme you have established for your Web site.

Step 9: Add the text given below and place it beneath the headline you entered in Step 8.

Format the text so that it is consistent with the style and design theme you have established for your Web site.

> In addition to our state-of-the-art weight training facility room, Ultimate Fitness offers a variety of aerobic, cardio, and personal training classes. This page is updated monthly. As a member, you can always check the class schedule online by visiting our Web site.
>
> Click here to visit our fitness class schedule online.

Note: You will be required to hyperlink the text that reads "*Click here to visit our fitness class schedule online*" above to the *Class Schedule* page, which you will create in Part 8 of the simulation.

Step 10: Add additional text and/or graphic images that help to enhance the professionalism and visual appeal of the Homepage.

You can access a variety of high-quality fitness images installed from the Ultimate Fitness Resource CD. The fitness images are located in the following directory:

<drive letter>:\Ultimate Fitness Resource CD\Fitness Images

Save any graphic images that you add to the *UF_Images* folder.

DESIGN TIP

Keep the size, style, and color of the text you enter consistent with the style and design theme you have established for your Web site.

RESOURCE CD

Consider using one or more of the fitness images available from the Ultimate Fitness Resource CD to enhance your Web site. The fitness images are installed in the following directory:

<drive letter>:\Ultimate Fitness Resource CD\ Fitness Images

Step 11: Hyperlink the navigation menu button titled *Home* to the Homepage (file name *"index"*).

IMPORTANT
STEP

Do not forget to
hyperlink the Home
menu button to the
Homepage.

Step 12: Save the file before moving on to the next part of the simulation.

Carefully review all the steps provided in this section to ensure you have included all the information required for the Homepage. Preview the Web site using your Internet browser and make any necessary changes before moving on to the next part of the simulation.

Part 4:
Design and Build the
Facilities Page

Approximate completion time for this section: 2-3 hours

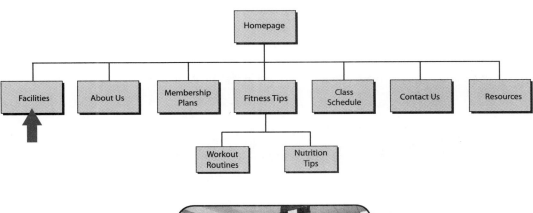

Part 4: Design and Build the Facilities Page

TASK AND PURPOSE:

- To design and build the Facilities page for the Ultimate Fitness Web site.
- The Facilities page will provide Web site visitors with a tour of the Ultimate Fitness facility by combining text and graphic images.

STRATEGIES AND DESIGN TIPS TO CONSIDER:

- Keep the text style, color, and size consistent throughout each page in your Web site.
- When entering the list of fitness equipment in Step 6, consider using bullets to make the list easy to read for Web site visitors. Also consider formatting the list into columns to avoid users having to scroll down the page to read the list.
- Before you begin building the Facilities page using your Web design software, read all of the instructions, information, and required content provided in this part of the simulation.
- Consider adding a picture caption to give meaning to any graphic images that you add to your Web site.
- Use the Web Page Planning Form to create a thumbnail sketch of the layout and design of your Facilities page.

INSTRUCTIONS, INFORMATION, AND REQUIRED CONTENT:

NOTE: Read all of the steps in this section before proceeding to Step 1 below.

Step 1: **With the Ultimate Fitness Web site open, do the following:**

1. Open the file "*index.*"
2. From the file menu of your software, choose *Save As* and rename the file "*facilities.*"

> **Note:** Opening the *index* file and saving it as *facilities* will allow you to quickly use the same formatting features that you used when creating the index file (homepage). This procedure will be used throughout the remainder of the simulation.

Step 2: **Add the following browser page title to the Facilities page:**

Ultimate Fitness: State-of-the-Art Health and Fitness Facilities

---

RESOURCE CD

Use the Web Page Planning Form installed from the Ultimate Fitness Resource CD to plan your Facilities page on paper before starting any work on the computer.

IMPORTANT STEP

Do not forget to add the browser page title to the Facilities page.

Step 3: **Add the following headline to the top area of the Facilities page:**

Welcome to the Facilities Tour of Ultimate Fitness

Format the text so that it is consistent with the style and design theme you have established for your Web site.

> **Note**: You may change the wording of the headline as long as it does not change its meaning or interpretation.

Step 4: **Add the text given below just beneath the headline you entered in Step 3 above.**

Format the text so that it is consistent with the style and design theme you have established for your Web site.

> The Ultimate Fitness state-of-the-art facility consists of more than 20,000 square feet of health and fitness equipment space. The facility features one free weight gym area, two aerobics rooms, a cardio room, a sauna room and Jacuzzi pool. We also have separate men's and women's locker rooms that contain lockers, changing rooms, and shower areas.

Step 5: **Add a graphic image that will visually illustrate the text you entered in Step 4 above.**

Consider using one of the fitness images available from the Ultimate Fitness Resource CD to enhance your Web site. The fitness images are installed in the following directory:

<drive letter>:\Ultimate Fitness Resource CD\Fitness Images

Save any graphic images that you add to the *UF_Images* folder.

DESIGN TIP

Keep the size, style, and color of the text you enter consistent with the style and design theme you have established for your Web site.

RESOURCE CD

Consider using one of the fitness images available from the Ultimate Fitness Resource CD to enhance your Web site. The fitness images are installed in the following directory:

<drive letter>:\Ultimate Fitness Resource CD\ Fitness Images

QUICK REFERENCE COLOR CHARTS

Ultimate Fitness RGB Web Color Chart				
Color	Blue	Black	Grey	White
Red (R)	18	0	102	255
Green (G)	52	0	102	255
Blue (B)	90	0	102	255

Ultimate Fitness Hexadecimal Values Web Color Chart	
Color	Hexadecimal Values
Blue	Hex={12, 34, 5A}
Black	Hex={00, 00, 00}
Grey	Hex={66, 66, 66}
White	Hex={FF, FF, FF}

Step 6: Add the headline and list of fitness equipment below to the Facilities page.

Format the text so that it is consistent with the style and design theme you have established for your Web site.

The Ultimate Fitness facility features the best in training, fitness equipment, and accommodations including:

Aerobics
Circuit Training
Elliptical Trainers
Free Weights
Group Cycling (Spinning)
Kickboxing
Men's and Women's Locker Rooms
Multi-screen Video System
Personal Training
Pilates
Plate-loaded Machines
Snack/Juice Bar
Stair Climbers
Stationary Cycling
Step Aerobics
Treadmills
Yoga

Step 7: Add additional text and/or graphic images that enhance the look and appearance of the Facilities page.

You can access a variety of high-quality fitness images installed from the Ultimate Fitness Resource CD. The fitness images are located in the following directory:

<drive letter>:\Ultimate Fitness Resource CD\Fitness Images

Save any graphic images that you add to the *UF_Images* folder.

Step 8: Hyperlink the navigation menu button titled *Facilities* to the Facilities page (file name *"facilities"*).

Step 9: Save the file before moving on to the next part of the simulation.

Carefully review all the steps provided in this section to ensure you have included all the information required for the Facilities page. Preview the Web site using your Internet browser and make any necessary changes before moving on to the next part of the simulation.

Part 5:
Design and Build the
About Us Page

Approximate completion time for this section: 1-2 hours

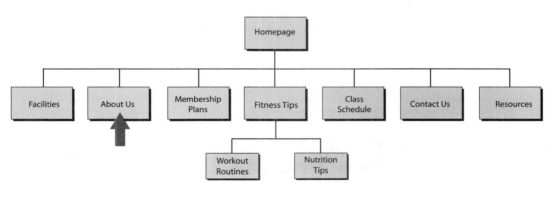

Part 5: Design and Build the About Us Page

TASK AND PURPOSE:

- To design and build the About Us page of the Ultimate Fitness Web site.
- The About Us page will provide Web site visitors with a more detailed overview of the history and background of the Ultimate Fitness establishment.

STRATEGIES AND DESIGN TIPS TO CONSIDER:

- Keep the size, color, and design of the text you will be adding to the About Us page consistent with those used on other pages of your Web site.
- When adding additional text and/or graphic images, be careful not to overcrowd the page.
- Use colors that are consistent with those provided in the Ultimate Fitness Web Color Charts.
- Before you begin building the About Us page using your Web design software, read all of the instructions, information, and required content provided in this part of the simulation.
- Use the Web Page Planning form to create a thumbnail sketch of the layout and design of your About Us page.

INSTRUCTIONS, INFORMATION, AND REQUIRED CONTENT:

NOTE: Read all of the steps in this section before proceeding to Step 1 below.

Step 1: **With the Ultimate Fitness Web site open, do the following:**

1. Open the file *"facilities."*
2. From the file menu of your software, choose *Save As* and rename the file *"about_us."*

Step 2: **Add the following browser page title to the About Us page:**

Ultimate Fitness: Read All About Us

Step 3:   **Add the following headline to the top area of the About Us page:**

Read All About Ultimate Fitness

Format the text so that it is consistent with the style and design theme you have established for your Web site.

Step 4:   **Add the text given below just beneath the headline you entered in Step 3.**

Format the text so that it is consistent with the style and design theme you have established for your Web site.

DESIGN TIP

Keep the size, style, and color of the text you enter consistent with the style and design theme you have established for your Web site.

Ultimate Fitness has an atmosphere that will make beginners feel right at home, yet there's enough equipment for high performance athletic training as well. We offer names including Cybex®, Hammer Strength®, Body Masters® and more.

We have no high-pressure sales people!

Our membership packages are flexible so you can sign up for a shorter term and not be locked into a long-term commitment. The people who sign you up are the same people you'll see every time you come in to work out.

Many of our member service representatives are also certified fitness trainers. This makes our staff able to help you whenever you need it, not just by appointment.

As part of your membership, you can sign up for free personal training sessions. To check the availability of our personal trainers, please click here to see our personal training and aerobics class schedule.

QUICK REFERENCE COLOR CHARTS

Ultimate Fitness RGB Web Color Chart				
Color	Blue	Black	Grey	White
Red (R)	18	0	102	255
Green (G)	52	0	102	255
Blue (B)	90	0	102	255

Ultimate Fitness Hexadecimal Values Web Color Chart	
Color	Hexadecimal Values
Blue	Hex={12, 34, 5A}
Black	Hex={00, 00, 00}
Grey	Hex={66, 66, 66}
White	Hex={FF, FF, FF}

HYPERLINK ALERT

Note: You will be required to hyperlink the text above that reads "*please click here to see our personal training and aerobics class schedule*" to the *Class Schedule* page, which you will create in Part 8 of the simulation.

Step 5: **Add additional text and/or graphic images that help to enhance the look and appearance of the About Us page.**

Consider using one or more of the fitness images available from the Ultimate Fitness Resource CD to enhance your Web site. The fitness images are installed in the following directory:

<drive letter>:\Ultimate Fitness Resource CD\Fitness Images

Save any graphic images that you add to the *UF_Images* folder.

Step 6: **Hyperlink the navigation menu button titled *About Us* to the About Us page (file name "*about_us*").**

Step 7: **Save the file before moving on to the next part of the simulation.**

RESOURCE CD

Consider using one or more of the fitness images available from the Ultimate Fitness Resource CD to enhance your Web site.

IMPORTANT STEP

Do not forget to hyperlink the About Us menu button to the About Us page.

✓ CHECK POINT

Carefully review all the steps provided in this section to ensure you have included all the information required for the About Us page. Preview the Web site using your Internet browser and make any necessary changes before moving on to the next part of the simulation.

Part 6:
Design and Build the Membership Plans Page

Approximate completion time for this section: 2-3 hours

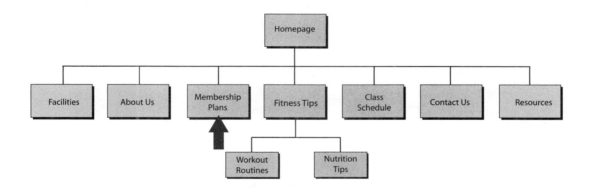

Part 6: Design and Build the Membership Plans Page

TASK AND PURPOSE:

- To design and build the Membership Plans page of the Ultimate Fitness Web site.
- The purpose of the Membership Plans page is to provide to non-member Web site visitors a description of the available membership plans, pricing, and specials available at Ultimate Fitness. The goal of this page is to attract new members to join Ultimate Fitness.

STRATEGIES AND DESIGN TIPS TO CONSIDER:

- Be sure to keep the size, color, and design of the text and graphics you add to the Membership Plans page consistent with the style and design theme you have established for your Web site.
- When entering the membership plans table in Step 6, be sure to place the text inside of a table to make the plans easier to read by Web site visitors.
- When formatting the membership plans table, consider filling the background of the cells with colors that match those given in the Ultimate Fitness color charts.
- Before you begin building the Membership Plans page using your Web design software, read all of the instructions, information, and required content provided in this part of the simulation.
- Use the Web Page Planning form to create a thumbnail sketch of the layout and design of your Membership Plans page.

RESOURCE CD

Use the Web Page Planning Form installed from the Ultimate Fitness Resource CD to plan your Membership Plans page on paper before starting any work on the computer.

INSTRUCTIONS, INFORMATION, AND REQUIRED CONTENT:

NOTE: Read all of the steps in this section before proceeding to step 1 below.

Step 1: With the Ultimate Fitness Web site open, do the following:

1. Open the file "*about_us.*"
2. From the file menu of your software, choose *Save As* and rename the file "*membership_plans.*"

Step 2: Add the following browser page title to the membership plans page:

Ultimate Fitness: Affordable Membership Plans

Step 3: Add the following headline to the top area of the Membership Plans page:

Ultimate Fitness has Membership Plans Available to Meet Any Budget

Format the text so that it is consistent with the style and design theme you have established for your Web site.

Step 4: Add the text given below just beneath the headline you entered in Step 3.

Format the text so that it is consistent with the style and design theme you have established for your Web site.

> Ultimate Fitness is dedicated to meeting your fitness goals. We offer several membership plans that are flexible and competitively priced to meet most budgets. With our try-before-you-buy specials, you can try Ultimate Fitness before committing to any membership plan.

IMPORTANT STEP

Do not forget to add the browser page title to the Membership Plans page.

DESIGN TIP

Keep the size, style, and color of the text you enter consistent with the style and design theme you have established for your Web site.

QUICK REFERENCE COLOR CHARTS

Ultimate Fitness RGB Web Color Chart			
Color	Blue	Black	Grey	White
Red (R)	18	0	102	255
Green (G)	52	0	102	255
Blue (B)	90	0	102	255

Ultimate Fitness Hexadecimal Values Web Color Chart	
Color	Hexadecimal Values
Blue	Hex={12, 34, 5A}
Black	Hex={00, 00, 00}
Grey	Hex={66, 66, 66}
White	Hex={FF, FF, FF}

Step 5: Add the following headline to the Membership Plans page:

Ultimate Fitness Offers Four Convenient Membership Plans

Format the text so that it is consistent with the style and design theme you have established for your Web site.

Step 6: Add the membership plans table shown in Table 6.1. Place the membership plans just below the headline you entered in Step 5 above.

Format the table so that it is consistent with the style and design theme you have established for your Web site.

DESIGN TIP

When formatting the membership plans table, consider filling the background of the cells with colors that match those given in the Ultimate Fitness color charts.

Table 6.1

Ultimate Fitness Membership Plans		
Plan	Description	Price
Monthly Plan	Pay your membership dues monthly and enjoy all the amenities and facilities at Ultimate Fitness.	$35.99 / month
Weekdays-Only Plan	Pay your membership dues monthly and enjoy all the amenities and facilities at Ultimate Fitness Monday through Friday only. Perfect if you do not plan to train on the weekends.	$29.99 / month
Six Month Plan	Join Ultimate Fitness for six months and save over 30% off of the monthly membership fee.	$149.00 / six months
Yearly Plan	Join Ultimate Fitness for one year and save over 40% off of the monthly membership fee.	$249.99 / year

Step 7: Insert the two VIP graphic images (file names *"VIP1"* and *"VIP2"*) that you created for the Homepage (Part 3, Step 6) on the Membership Plans page.

Step 8: **Add the following text to the Membership Plans page:**

Have a question about joining Ultimate Fitness?

Please see our Contact Us page to find out how
to reach us or call 1.888.757.4856.

Note: You will be required to hyperlink the text that reads
"Contact Us" above to the contact us page, which you will create
in Part 9 of the simulation.

Step 9: **Add additional text and/or graphic images that help to enhance the look and appearance of the Membership Plans page.**

Consider using one of the fitness images available from the Ultimate Fitness Resource CD. The fitness images are installed in the following directory:

<drive letter>:\Ultimate Fitness Resource CD\Fitness Images

Save any graphic images that you add to the *UF_Images* folder.

RESOURCE CD

Consider using one
or more of the fitness
images available
from the Ultimate
Fitness Resource CD to
enhance your Web site.

Step 10: **Hyperlink the "New Member Specials" button, starburst, or callout graphic (previously created Part 2-A, Step 6) housed in the top shared navigation area to the Membership Plans page.**

IMPORTANT STEP

Do not forget to
hyperlink the "New
Member Specials"
graphic image to
the Membership
Plans page.

Step 11: **Open the Homepage (file name "*index*") and hyperlink the two VIP passes from the Homepage to the Membership Plans page.**

IMPORTANT STEP

Do not forget to
hyperlink the VIP
passes on the
Homepage to the
Membership Plans
page.

Step 12: Open the Homepage (file name *"index"*) and hyperlink the text that reads "Membership Plans" (Part 3, Step 4) to the Membership Plans page (file name *"membership_plans"*).

Step 13: Hyperlink the navigation menu button titled *Membership Plans* to the Membership Plans page (file name *"membership_plans"*).

Step 14: Save the file before moving on to the next part of the simulation.

Carefully review all the steps provided in this section to ensure you have included all the information required for the Membership Plans page. Preview the Web site using your Internet browser and make any necessary changes before moving on to the next part of the simulation.

Part 7:
Design and Build the
Fitness Tips Pages

Approximate completion time for this section: 4-6 hours

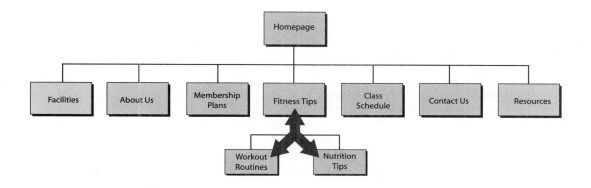

This part of the simulation is divided into the following three sub-parts:

Part 7-A: Design and build the Fitness Tips main page
Part 7-B: Design and build the Workout Routines page
Part 7-C: Design and build the Nutrition Tips page

Introduction to Part 7:
Design and Build the Fitness Tips Pages

Part 7 of the simulation is divided into three sub-parts: 7-A, 7-B and 7-C. In these three sub-parts, you will be asked to create three different pages. A Fitness Tips main page which will be hyperlinked to two separate sub-pages (see Figure 7.1). Web site visitors can access the Fitness Tips main page and then choose to click on two hyperlinks to access the Workout Routines page or the Nutrition Tips page.

The three pages you will build in Part 7 are as follows:

Part 7-A: Design and Build the Fitness Tips Main Page
Part 7-B: Design and Build the Workout Routines Page
Part 7-C: Design and Build the Nutrition Tips Page

Figure 7.1: Outline of the Fitness Tips Pages

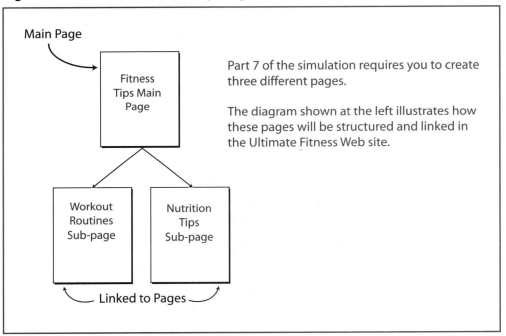

Main Page

Fitness Tips Main Page

Part 7 of the simulation requires you to create three different pages.

The diagram shown at the left illustrates how these pages will be structured and linked in the Ultimate Fitness Web site.

Workout Routines Sub-page

Nutrition Tips Sub-page

Linked to Pages

Part 7-A: Design and Build the Fitness Tips Main Page

TASK AND PURPOSE:

- To design and build the Fitness Tips main page.
- The purpose of the Fitness Tips main page is to provide Web site visitors with fitness-related tips and information. Providing this type of page helps to enhance the overall quality and professional image of the Ultimate Fitness establishment.

STRATEGIES AND DESIGN TIPS TO CONSIDER:

- Keep the size, color, and design of the text you enter consistent with the style and design theme you established in your Web site.
- Before you begin building the Fitness Tips main page using your Web design software, read all of the instructions, information, and required content provided in this part of the simulation.
- Keep the size of any graphic images that you add consistent with those on other pages within your Web site.
- Use the Web Page Planning form to create a thumbnail sketch of the layout and design of your Fitness Tips main page.

INSTRUCTIONS, INFORMATION, AND REQUIRED CONTENT:

NOTE: Read all of the steps in this section before proceeding to Step 1 below.

Step 1: **With the Ultimate Fitness Web site open, do the following:**

1. Open the file "*membership_plans.*"
2. From the file menu of your software, choose *Save As* and rename the file "*fitness_tips_main.*"

Step 2: **Add the following browser page title to the Fitness Tips main page:**

Ultimate Fitness: Offering Expert Fitness Tips and Advice

RESOURCE CD

Use the Web Page Planning Form installed from the Ultimate Fitness Resource CD to plan your Fitness Tips main page on paper before starting any work on the computer.

IMPORTANT STEP

Do not forget to add the browser page title to the Fitness Tips main page.

Step 3: Add the following headline to the top area of the Fitness Tips main page:

Access FREE Fitness Tips from the Ultimate Fitness Personal Trainers

Format the text so that it is consistent with the style and design theme you have established for your Web site.

Step 4: Add the text given below beneath the headline you entered in Step 3.

Format the text so that it is consistent with the style and design theme you have established for your Web site.

> To help our members maximize their health and fitness goals, Ultimate Fitness provides some of the best personal trainers in the industry. Combined, our personal trainers have over 100 years of fitness, diet, and exercise experience. Our personal trainers regularly provide free training classes and are also available for private training sessions.
>
> Click on one of the two links below to access our free fitness tips and advice:
>
> 1. Weightlifting Workout Routines
> 2. Nutrition Tips

 Note: You will be required to hyperlink the text that reads "*1. Weightlifting Workout Routines*" and "*2. Nutrition Tips*" later in this part of the simulation.

Step 5: Add additional text and/or graphic images to enhance the look and appearance of the Fitness Tips main page.

Consider using one of the fitness images available from the Ultimate Fitness Resource CD. The fitness images are installed in the following directory:

<drive letter>:\Ultimate Fitness Resource CD\Fitness Images

Save any graphic images that you add to the *UF_Images* folder.

Step 6: Hyperlink the navigation menu button titled *Fitness Tips* to the Fitness Tips main page (file name "*fitness_tips_main*").

IMPORTANT STEP

Do not forget to hyperlink the Fitness Tips menu button to the Fitness Tips main page.

Step 7: Save the file before moving on to the next part of the simulation.

✓ CHECK POINT

Carefully review all the steps provided in this section to ensure you have included all the information required for the Fitness Tips main page. Preview the Web site using your Internet browser and make any necessary changes before moving on to the next part of the simulation.

Part 7-B: Design and Build the Workout Routines Page

TASK AND PURPOSE:

- To design and build the Workout Routines page.
- The Workout Routines page will provide Web site visitors with a variety of basic weightlifting routines. This page is the first sub-page of the fitness tips main page.

STRATEGIES AND DESIGN TIPS TO CONSIDER:

- Keep the size, color, and design of the text you enter consistent with the style and design theme you established in your Web site.
- Consider adding a picture caption to give meaning to any graphic images that you add to your Web site.
- Before you begin building the Workout Routines page using your Web design software, read all of the instructions, information, and required content provided in this part of the simulation.
- Use the Web Page Planning form to create a thumbnail sketch of the layout and design of your Workout Routines page.

INSTRUCTIONS, INFORMATION, AND REQUIRED CONTENT:

NOTE: Read all of the steps in this section before proceeding to Step 1 below.

Step 1: **With the Ultimate Fitness Web site open, do the following:**

1. Open the file "*fitness_tips_main.*"
2. From the file menu of your software, choose *Save As* and rename the file "*workout_routines.*"

Step 2: **Add the following browser page title to the Workout Routines page:**

Ultimate Fitness: Workout Routines

RESOURCE CD

Use the Web Page Planning Form installed from the Ultimate Fitness Resource CD to plan your Workout Routines page on paper before starting any work on the computer.

IMPORTANT STEP

Do not forget to add the browser page title to the Workout Routines page.

Step 3: **Add the article shown in Table 7.1 titled *"Introduction to Working Out With Weights"* to the Workout Routines page.**

Read the article first before placing it on the workout routines page. You may change the format and layout of the text in the article to make it easier to read and more appealing to Web site visitors. Keep the format of the text consistent with the style and design of your Web site.

Step 4: **Add one or more graphic images to help enhance the look and appearance of the article you entered in Step 3 above.**

Consider using one of the fitness images available from the Ultimate Fitness Resource CD. The fitness images are installed in the following directory:

<drive letter>:\Ultimate Fitness Resource CD\Fitness Images

Save any graphic images that you add to the *UF_Images* folder.

Step 5: **Using your Web graphic design software, create a "Back to the Fitness Tips Main Page" graphic image button.**

This button will allow Web site visitors to easily navigate back to the Fitness Tips main page. You may shorten the text on the button as long as it does not change its meaning. For example, you can create the button to simply read "Back."

Save the button as *"Back_to_fitness"* in the *"UF_Buttons"* folder.

Step 6: **Insert the button you created in Step 5 above in both the top and bottom areas of the Workout Routines page.**

Step 7: **Hyperlink the button you placed in Step 6 above to the Fitness Tips main page (file name *"fitness_tips_main"*).**

Step 8: **Open the Fitness Tips main page (file name *"fitness_tips_main"*) and hyperlink the text that reads *"1. Weightlifting Workout Routines"* (from Part 7-A, Step 4) to the Workout Routines page (file name *"workout_routines"*).**

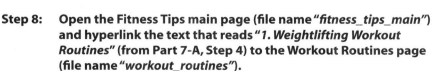

QUICK REFERENCE COLOR CHARTS

Ultimate Fitness RGB Web Color Chart				
Color	Blue	Black	Grey	White
Red (R)	18	0	102	255
Green (G)	52	0	102	255
Blue (B)	90	0	102	255

Ultimate Fitness Hexadecimal Values Web Color Chart	
Color	Hexadecimal Values
Blue	Hex={12, 34, 5A}
Black	Hex={00, 00, 00}
Grey	Hex={66, 66, 66}
White	Hex={FF, FF, FF}

Table 7.1

Introduction to Working Out With Weights

One rule when making weightlifting workout programs is to make sure to split it so that you aren't over-training. Doing chest on Monday, then triceps on Tuesday, then shoulders on Wednesday will overtrain your triceps. Why? Because just about every chest and shoulder exercise works the triceps secondary. And, almost every back exercise works the biceps secondary. So, you would need to do one of three things when making your workout routines and splits:

1) Work chest, triceps and shoulders on the same day, and biceps and back on the same day so that it's okay if the secondary muscles get worked that day, because you're doing them anyway.

2) Separate those muscles that work a secondary muscle so that they are far enough apart not to overtrain you. For example, do chest and biceps Monday, triceps Wednesday, and shoulders and back Friday.

3) Do chest and triceps Monday, and shoulders Thursday, and back and biceps together on Friday.

While there are a variety of weightlifting routines available, a very popular routine is a split routine where you work different body parts on alternating days of the week. A sample split routine is shown below.

Sample Split Routine

Monday/Thursday – Chest, Triceps, and Biceps

Chest
Flat Bench Press - 4 sets
Incline Hammer Strength Machine - 2 sets
Dumbell Flyes - 2 sets

Triceps
Tricep Press down - 2 sets
Dips (weighted) - 2 sets

Biceps
Standing Barbell Curls - 3 sets
Barbell Preacher Curls - 2 sets

Wednesday – Cardio
Treadmill – 20 minutes
Elliptical trainer – 20 minutes

Tuesday/Friday – Back and Legs

Back
Barbell upright rows - 3 sets
Lat Pull downs - 3 sets
Seated Cable Row - 2 sets

Legs
Squats - 4 sets
Leg Extension - 2 sets
Leg Curl - 2 sets
Seated or standing calve raises - 3 sets

Shoulders
Seated Dumbbell Military Press - 4 sets
Lateral Raises - 3 sets
Shrugs - 3 sets

Saturday/Sunday - days off

See an Ultimate Fitness personal trainer for advice on what routine works best for you.

Source: Reprinted with permission from Fitness and Freebies Newsletter (*http://www.fitnessandfreebies.com*).

Step 9: Save the file before moving on to the next part of the simulation.

Carefully review all the steps provided in this section to ensure you have included all the information required for the Workout Routines page. Preview the Web site using your Internet browser and make any necessary changes before moving on to the next part of the simulation.

Part 7-C: Design and Build the Nutrition Tips Page

TASK AND PURPOSE:

- To design and build the Nutrition Tips page.
- The Nutrition Tips page will provide Web site visitors with an informational article related to the benefits of physical activity. This page is the second sub-page of the fitness tips main page.

STRATEGIES AND DESIGN TIPS TO CONSIDER:

- Keep the size, color, and design of the text you enter consistent with the style and design theme you established in your Web site.
- Before you begin building the Nutrition Tips page using your Web design software, read all of the instructions, information, and required content provided in this part of the simulation.
- Consider adding a picture caption to give meaning to any graphic images that you add to your Web site.
- Use colors that are consistent with those provided in the Ultimate Fitness Web Color Charts.
- Use the Web Page Planning form to create a thumbnail sketch of the layout and design of your Nutrition Tips page.

INSTRUCTIONS, INFORMATION, AND REQUIRED CONTENT:

NOTE: Read all of the steps in this section before proceeding to Step 1 below.

Step 1: **With the Ultimate Fitness Web site open, do the following:**

1. Open the file "*workout_routines*."
2. From the file menu of your software, choose *Save As* and rename the file "*nutrition_tips*."

Step 2: **Add the following browser page title to the Nutrition Tips page:**

Ultimate Fitness: Nutrition Tips

RESOURCE CD

Use the Web Page Planning Form installed from the Ultimate Fitness Resource CD to plan your Nutrition Tips page on paper before starting any work on the computer.

IMPORTANT STEP

Do not forget to add the browser page title to the Nutrition Tips page.

Step 3: **Add the article shown in Table 7.2 titled *"Introduction to Physical Fitness and Nutrition"* to the Nutrition Tips page.**

Read the article first before placing it on the nutrition tips page. You may change the format and layout of the text in the article to make it easier to read and more appealing to Web site visitors. Keep the format of the text consistent with the style and design of your Web site.

DESIGN TIP

Consider changing the layout of the text in the article shown in table 7.2 to make it easier to read for Web site visitors.

Step 4: **Add additional graphic images to enhance the look and appearance of the article you entered in Step 3 above.**

Consider using one of the fitness images available from the Ultimate Fitness Resource CD. The fitness images are installed in the following directory:

<drive letter>:\Ultimate Fitness Resource CD\Fitness Images

Save any graphic images that you add to the *UF_Images* folder.

RESOURCE CD

Consider using one or more of the fitness images available from the Ultimate Fitness Resource CD to enhance your Web site.

Step 5: **Insert the button you created in Part 7-B, Step 5 (file name *"Back_to_fitness"*) in both the top and bottom areas of the Nutrition Tips page.**

Step 6: **Hyperlink the button you placed in Step 5 above to the Fitness Tips main page (file name *fitness_tips_main*).**

IMPORTANT STEP

Step 7: **Open the Fitness Tips main page (file name *fitness_tips_main*) and hyperlink the text that reads *"2. Nutrition Tips"* (from Part 7-A, Step 4) to the Nutrition Tips page (file name *nutrition_tips*).**

Pay close attention to the hyperlink instructions given in Steps 6 and 7.

Step 8: **Save the file before moving on to the next part of the simulation.**

Table 7.2

Introduction to Physical Fitness and Nutrition

For years everyone has known that regular exercise along with good nutrition is good for his or her health. The trick is how to build sound exercise habits and a balanced diet into your busy schedule. The stress of modern times mandates that you develop and maintain a fit, trim, and fully functioning body. Being active and physically fit heightens your self-expression and self-esteem.

Research polls indicate that people today are becoming more health centered. As a result, people are becoming more interested in making fitness exercise an integral part of their lifestyle. This article will introduce you to the *why* of fitness. You will learn all about exercise and its benefits and will also learn how to structure a personal exercise program that is safe, reasonable, effective, and, most important, rewarding and fun.

Give some thought to the following statements:

- In the past, health meant only absence of disease. Today we have a much broader perspective and consider physical fitness to be a key component of total health.

- The modern lifestyle fosters unfitness because technological advances have eliminated much fitness producing physical exertion from everyday activities.

- Everyday activities, even for the laborer, no longer adequately stimulate the heart, lungs, and muscles to produce physiological benefits.

- Society, especially the corporate world, is beginning to realize the importance of health promotion and the role of exercise in developing and maintaining good health habits.

- Being physically fit means living at your fullest physical potential. Physical fitness is the capability of the heart, blood vessels, lungs, and muscles to function at optimal efficiency. It provides a basis for living a full and rewarding life.

- The basic health components of physical fitness are cardio-respiratory endurance, strength, muscular endurance, flexibility, and body composition.

- To be physically fit does take effort (yes, some sweat, too!), but exercise does not have to be punishing to help you develop and maintain physical fitness.

- Regular and vigorous exercise of the total body is a necessary ingredient of muscular and circulatory fitness - the key to good health and well-being.

Source: Reprinted with permission from Fitness and Freebies Newsletter (*http://www.fitnessandfreebies.com*).

Carefully review all the steps provided in this section to ensure you have included all the information required for the Nutrition Tips page. Preview the Web site using your Internet browser and make any necessary changes before moving on to the next part of the simulation.

Part 8:
Design and Build the
Class Schedule Page

Approximate completion time for this section: 1-2 hours

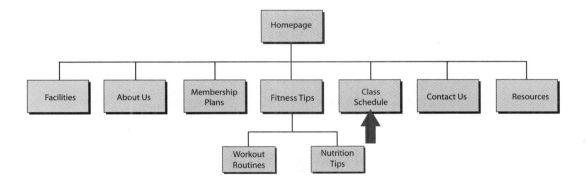

Part 8: Design and Build the Class Schedule Page

TASK AND PURPOSE:

- To design and build the Class Schedule page of the Ultimate Fitness Web site.
- The purpose of the Class Schedule page is to provide both members and non-members of Ultimate Fitness online access to the aerobic, cardio, and personal training schedule.

STRATEGIES AND DESIGN TIPS TO CONSIDER:

- Keep the size, color, and design of the text you enter consistent with the style and design theme you established in your Web site.
- Use colors that are consistent with those provided in the Ultimate Fitness Web Color Charts.
- Format the class schedule table (shown in Table 8.1) using the same text and color scheme that you have established for your Web site.
- Before you begin building the Class Schedule page using your Web design software, read all of the instructions, information, and required content provided in this part of the simulation.
- Use the Web Page Planning form to create a thumbnail sketch of the layout and design of your Class Schedule page.

INSTRUCTIONS, INFORMATION, AND REQUIRED CONTENT:

NOTE: Read all of the steps in this section before proceeding to Step 1 below.

Step 1: **With the Ultimate Fitness Web site open, do the following:**

1. Open the file "*nutrition_tips.*"
2. From the file menu of your software, choose *Save As* and rename the file "*class_schedule.*"

Step 2: **Add the following browser page title to the Class Schedule page:**

Ultimate Fitness: Schedule of Classes

RESOURCE CD

Use the Web Page Planning Form installed from the Ultimate Fitness Resource CD to plan your Class Schedule page on paper before starting any work on the computer.

IMPORTANT STEP

Do not forget to add the browser page title to the Class Schedule page.

Step 3: **Add the following headline to the top of the Class Schedule page:**

The Ultimate Fitness Class Schedule

Format the text so that it is consistent with the style and design theme you have established for your Web site.

DESIGN TIP

Keep the size, style, and color of the text you enter consistent with the style and design theme you have established for your Web site.

Step 4: **Add the text given below just beneath the headline you entered in Step 3.**

Included on this page is our weekly aerobic, cardio, and personal training schedule. Our schedule is updated monthly, so please check this page often for updates.

Format the text so that it is consistent with the style and design theme you have established for your Web site.

Step 5: **Add the class schedule shown in Table 8.1 to the Class Schedule page. Enter all the text exactly as shown.**

Format the class schedule table so that it is consistent with the style and design theme you have established for your Web site.

DESIGN TIP

Format the class schedule table (shown in Table 8.1) using the same text and color scheme that you have established thus far in your Web site.

Step 6: **Open the Homepage (file name "*index*") and hyperlink the text that reads "*Click here to visit our fitness class schedule online*" (from Part 3, Step 9) to the Class Schedule page.**

Step 7: **Open the About Us page (file name "*about_us*") and hyperlink the text that reads "*please click here to see our personal training and aerobics class schedule*" (from Part 5, Step 4) to the Class Schedule page.**

IMPORTANT STEP

Pay close attention to the hyperlink instructions given in Steps 6 and 7.

Table 8.1

Ultimate Fitness Weekly Aerobic and Personal Training Schedule
Note: Please visit this page monthly as the schedule is updated on the first day of each month.

Time	Monday	Tuesday	Wednesday	Thursday	Friday	Saturday	Sunday
7:00 - 8:00 a.m.	Low-Impact Aerobics	Total Yoga	Trekking	Low-Impact Aerobics	Total Yoga	X	X
8:00 - 9:00 a.m.	Trekking	Cardio Kickboxing	Aerobic Hip-hop Dancing	Total Yoga	Cardio Kickboxing	Trekking	Low-Impact Aerobics
9:00 - 10:00 a.m.	Total Yoga	Spinning	Trekking	Aerobic Hip-hop Dancing	Spinning	Cardio Kickboxing	Trekking
10:00 - 11:00 a.m.	High-Impact Aerobics	Power Up Pump	Total Yoga	Power Up Pump	Aerobic Hip-hop Dancing	Spinning	Pilates
4:00 - 5:00 p.m.	Aerobic Hip-hop Dancing	Power Up Pump	Total Yoga	Trekking	Total Yoga	Aerobic Hip-hop Dancing	Cardio Kickboxing
5:00 - 6:00 p.m.	High-Impact Aerobics	Power Up Pump	Cardio Kickboxing	High-Impact Aerobics	Cardio Kickboxing	Power Up Pump	X
6:00 - 7:00 p.m	Pilates	Cardio Kickboxing	Aerobic Hip-hop Dancing	Pilates	Power Up Pump	X	X
7:00 - 8:00 p.m.	Trekking	Low-Impact Aerobics	Cardio Kickboxing	Cardio Kickboxing	High-Impact Aerobics	X	X

X = No class offered for the given time slot
Personal training is available during all time slots shown above.

Step 8: Hyperlink the navigation menu button titled *Class Schedule* to the Class Schedule page (file name *"class_schedule"*).

Step 9: Save the file before moving on to the next part of the simulation.

IMPORTANT STEP

Do not forget to hyperlink the Class Schedule menu button to the Class Schedule page.

✓CHECK POINT

Carefully review all the steps provided in this section to ensure you have included all the information required for the Class Schedule page. Preview the Web site using your Internet browser and make any necessary changes before moving on to the next part of the simulation.

Part 9:
Design and Build the Contact Us Page

Approximate completion time for this section: 1-2 hours

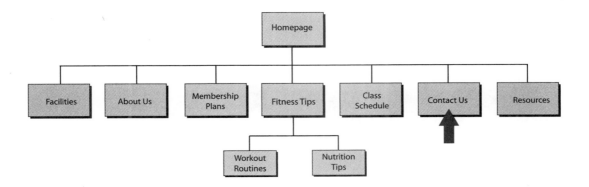

Part 9: Design and Build the Contact Us Page

TASK AND PURPOSE:

- To design and build the Contact Us page of the Ultimate Fitness Web site.
- The purpose of the Contact Us page is to provide Web site visitors with the Ultimate Fitness address, phone number, fax number, e-mail address, and the hours of operation.

STRATEGIES AND DESIGN TIPS TO CONSIDER:

- Keep the size, color, and design of the text you enter consistent with the style and design theme you established in your Web site.
- Before you begin building the Contact Us page using your Web design software, read all of the instructions, information, and required content provided in this part of the simulation.
- Use the Web Page Planning form to create a thumbnail sketch of the layout and design of your Contact Us page.

INSTRUCTIONS, INFORMATION, AND REQUIRED CONTENT:

NOTE: Read all of the steps in this section before proceeding to Step 1 below.

Step 1: With the Ultimate Fitness Web site open, do the following:

1. Open the file "class_schedule."
2. From the file menu of your software, choose *Save As* and rename the file "*contact_us.*"

Step 2: Add the following browser page title to the Contact Us page:

Ultimate Fitness: Contact Us

RESOURCE CD

Use the Web Page Planning Form installed from the Ultimate Fitness Resource CD to plan your Contact Us page on paper before starting any work on the computer.

IMPORTANT STEP

Do not forget to add the browser page title to the Contact Us page.

Step 3: Add the following headline to the top of the Contact Us page:

How to Reach Ultimate Fitness

Format the text so that it is consistent with the style and design theme you have established for your Web site.

Step 4: Add the text given below beneath the headline you entered in Step 3.

Format the text so that it is consistent with the style and design theme you have established for your Web site.

You may contact us using any of the methods indicated below. We welcome any questions, comments, suggestions, or feedback.

Ultimate Fitness
350 Park Avenue
New York, NY 10019
Phone: 1.888.757.4856
Fax: 1.888.757.4987
E-mail: contact@uf-online.com

Hours of Operation:
Monday – Friday 7 am – 10 pm
Saturday 8 am – 6 pm
Sunday 8 am – 5 pm

Step 5: Hyperlink the e-mail address you entered in Step 4 *(contact@uf-online.com)* so that when a site visitor clicks on the e-mail address, an e-mail software program will automatically open to send an e-mail message to Ultimate Fitness.

Step 6: Open the Membership Plans page (file name *"membership_plans"*) and hyperlink the text that reads *"Contact Us"* (Part 6, Step 8) to the Contact Us page.

DESIGN TIP

Keep the size, style, and color of the text you enter consistent with the style and design theme you have established for your Web site.

IMPORTANT STEP

Pay close attention to the hyperlink instructions given in Steps 5 and 6.

Step 7: **Add additional text and/or grapic images to enhance the appearance and professionalism of the Contact Us page.**

Consider using one or more of the fitness images installed from the Ultimate Fitness Resource CD. The fitness images are installed in the following directory:

<drive letter>:\Ultimate Fitness Resource CD\Fitness Images

Save any graphic images that you add to the *UF_Images* folder.

Step 8: **Hyperlink the navigation menu button titled *Contact Us* to the Contact Us page (file name "*contact_us*").**

Step 9: **Save the file before moving on to the next part of the simulation.**

RESOURCE CD

Consider using one or more of the fitness images available from the Ultimate Fitness Resource CD to enhance your Web site.

IMPORTANT STEP

Do not forget to hyperlink the Contact Us menu button to the Contact Us page.

Carefully review all the steps provided in this section to ensure you have included all the information required for the Contact Us page. Preview the Web site using your Internet browser and make any necessary changes before moving on to the next part of the simulation.

Part 10:
Design and Build the
Resources Page

Approximate completion time for this section: 2-3 hours

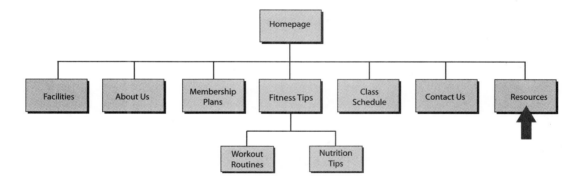

Part 10: Design and Build the Resources Page

TASK AND PURPOSE:

- To design and build the Resources page of the Ultimate Fitness Web site.
- The purpose of the Resources page is to provide links to health and fitness-related Web sites to Web site visitors. Providing additional resources enhances the professional image of Ultimate Fitness. It further demonstrates the establishment's commitment to providing the tools and resources necessary to help its members achieve their personal health and fitness goals.

STRATEGIES AND DESIGN TIPS TO CONSIDER:

- Keep the size, color, and design of the text you enter consistent with the style and design theme you established in your Web site.
- When entering the list of resources (shown in Table 10.1), keep the format and style of the text and hyperlinks consistent with other tables you have added to the Web site.
- Before you begin building the Resources page using your Web design software, read all of the instructions, information, and required content provided in this part of the simulation.
- Use the Web Page Planning form to create a thumbnail sketch of the layout and design of your Resources page.

INSTRUCTIONS, INFORMATION, AND REQUIRED CONTENT:

NOTE: Read all of the steps in this section before proceeding to Step 1 below.

Step 1: **With the Ultimate Fitness Web site open, do the following:**

1. Open the file "contact_us."
2. From the file menu of your software, choose *Save As* and rename the file "*resources.*"

Step 2: **Add the following browser page title to the Resources page:**

Ultimate Fitness: Health and Fitness Resources

RESOURCE CD

Use the Web Page Planning Form installed from the Ultimate Fitness Resource CD to plan your Resources page on paper before starting any work on the computer.

IMPORTANT STEP

Do not forget to add the browser page title to the Resources page.

Step 3: **Add the following headline to the top of the Resources page:**

Health and Fitness Resources

Format the text so that it is consistent with the style and design theme you have established for your Web site.

Step 4: **Add the text given below beneath the headline you entered in Step 3.**

Format the text so that it is consistent with the style and design theme you have established for your Web site.

> To help you achieve your health and fitness goals, Ultimate Fitness has reviewed and certifies that the Web sites shown below are highly credible online resources. The following are links to these Web sites:

Step 5: **Add the text shown in Table 10.1 below the text you added in Step 4 above. Hyperlink each Web site title to its respective Web site address provided in the column labeled "*Web Site Address*."**

Note: Be sure to double-check your hyperlinks to ensure that they are linked and are working properly.

Step 6: **Add one or more graphic image(s) to enhance the appearance and professionalism of the Resources page.**

Consider using one or more of the fitness images installed from the Ultimate Fitness Resource CD. The fitness images are installed in the following directory:

<drive letter>:\Ultimate Fitness Resource CD\Fitness Images

Save any graphic images that you add to the *UF_Images* folder.

Step 7: **Hyperlink the navigation menu button titled *Resources* to the Resources page (file name "*resources*").**

Step 8: **Save the file.**

DESIGN TIP

Keep the size, style, and color of the text you enter consistent with the style and design theme you have established for your Web site.

IMPORTANT STEP

Double-check the hyperlinks you add from table 10.1

IMPORTANT STEP

Do not forget to hyperlink the Resources menu button to the Resources page.

Table 10.1

Health and Fitness Web Site Resources Provided by Ultimate Fitness		
Web Site Title	Description	Web Site Address
Active Wellness and Fitness	Dedicated to providing health and fitness resources, tips, and tools to the residents of Massachusetts and beyond.	http://www.wellness.ma/
All Spirit Fitness	Brings a holistic, mind-body-spirit approach to both traditional and alternative fitness and exercise.	http://www.allspiritfitness.com/
Bodybuilding4u.com	Provides advice, tips, and articles on fitness, health, workout routines, diet and nutrition.	http://www.bodybuilding4u.com/
ExRx.net	Resource for the exercise professional, coach, or fitness enthusiast. Features an extensive exercise and muscle directory.	http://www.exrx.net/
Firstpath.com	Health and fitness information for the mind, body, and soul.	http://www.firstpath.com/
Fitness Library	Offers various approaches to weight management, book and fitness equipment reviews, and a guide to evaluating one's lifestyle.	http://www.primusweb.com/fitnesspartner/library/libindex.htm
Fitness Online	Features updated features on nutrition, training, health, fitness, and more from a variety of sources including Shape, Muscle & Fitness, and Men's Fitness magazines.	http://www.fitnessonline.com/
Fitness2live	Offering personalized, interactive fitness, diet, and health services, information, and tools.	http://www.fitness2live.com.au/
FitMoves	Featuring choreography exchanges, video clips, spinning database, and personal training tips.	http://www.fitmoves.com/
Health & Fitness Tips	Specializing in health and fitness information including weight loss, diet, and nutrition.	http://www.health-fitness-tips.com/
Intense Workout	Information about weightlifting, weight loss and gain, workout routines, diet, and exercise.	http://www.intense-workout.com/
Just Move	Physical fitness news, forums, exercise diaries, getting started tips, and more from the American Heart Association.	http://www.justmove.org/
Natural Physiques	Provides health and wellness articles and tools related to training, nutrition, and the personal development aspect of living healthy.	http://www.naturalphysiques.com
Netfit	Provides information for fitness, health, and exercise. Also includes abdominal and stretching exercises, food facts, and fitness tips.	http://www.netfit.co.uk/
President's Council on Physical Fitness and Sports (PCPFS)	Serves to promote, encourage, and motivate Americans of all ages to become physically active and participate in sports.	http://www.fitness.gov/
Shape Up America	Provides information about safe weight management and physical fitness.	http://www.shapeup.org/
Small Steps to Better Health	Offers tips and encouragement to help people learn how to eat better and live healthier lives. From the U.S. Department of Health & Human Services.	http://www.smallstep.gov/
Tude Fitness	Features exercise tips, running information, recipes, and more.	http://www.tudefitness.com/
WebGuru: Fitness Articles	Provides fitness articles on everything from exercises to body sculpting.	http://www.webguru.com/fitness-general/
Workouts That Work	Includes exercise and nutrition guidelines, and printable workouts.	http://workoutsthatwork.com
World Fitness	Free answers from personal trainers and exercise experts, free photo album, Bobbie's bodacious abs, and more.	http://www.fitwise.com/worldfitness/

Carefully review all the steps provided in this section to ensure you have included all the information required for the Resources page. Preview the Web site using your Internet browser and make any necessary changes before moving on to the next part of the simulation.

Congratulations!

Your Ultimate Fitness Web Site is Now Complete!

Congratulations!

You have successfully completed the Ultimate Fitness Web Site Design Simulation!

Using the Web site you have just completed, Ultimate Fitness can now enjoy a professional Web presence to advertise and showcase to its current members and potential new members.

Use the checklist provided below before submitting your Web site to your instructor for evaluation and grading.

Final Web Site Checklist
☑ The design of each page in your Web site is consistent in style, color, text, and graphic images.
☑ The text is consistent in size, color, and style throughout the Web site.
☑ All hyperlinks are working properly and are linked to the proper pages.
☑ All required information and elements have been included on each page.
☑ The Web site is free of any grammatical and spelling errors.
☑ The navigation areas are visible on all pages of the Web site.
☑ All information and page elements display properly when the Web site is viewed using an Internet browser.

In addition to the checklist shown above, before you submit your Web site to your instructor for evaluation and grading, it's a good idea to have two or three classmates review the Web site for content and design. A second set of eyes will often find design flaws or spelling errors that you were not able to find.